OLYMPIC VISIONS

IMAGES OF THE GAMES THROUGH HISTORY

MIKE O'MAHONY

REAKTION BOOKS

To the wonderful and unique institution that is the National Health Service

Published by Reaktion Books Ltd
33 Great Sutton Street
London EC1V 0DX, UK

First published 2012
Copyright © Mike O'Mahony 2012

Printed and bound in China

British Library Cataloguing in Publication Data
O'Mahony, Mike.
    Olympic visions : images of the Games through history.
    1. Olympics in art.
    2. Olympics — Collectibles--History.
    I. Title
    704.9'4979648–DC23

ISBN 978 1 86189 910 1

CONTENTS

2,008 drummers performing during the opening ceremony at the Beijing Olympic Games, 8 August 2008.

INTRODUCTION: OLYMPIC VISIONS

In August 2008 91,000 spectators, including over 100 heads of state, packed into the newly built National Stadium in Beijing to witness one of the most spectacular mass theatrical events ever staged.[1] The opening ceremony at the Beijing Olympic Games certainly outshone all its predecessors in terms of sheer grandeur and theatricality. At precisely 8 p.m. on the eighth day of the eighth month of the eighth year of the new millennium – eight being a lucky number in Chinese culture – an estimated television audience of around three billion, or approaching half of the world's entire population, tuned in as 2,008 drummers, dressed as ancient warriors yet wielding LED illuminated drumsticks, began the show by pounding out a rhythm that symbolically welcomed the world to Beijing. Over the course of the next four hours, over 10,000 carefully choreographed performers enacted a celebration of Chinese history and cultural achievements, from Confucian philosophy to the invention of printing.[2] Following the conventional parade of the athletes, the ceremony culminated with Chinese gymnast Li Ning carrying the Olympic torch around the stadium at roof height, borne aloft by invisible wires, before igniting the Olympic cauldron to mass cheers. The spectacle, estimated to have cost around $100 million (£62.5 million), had been carefully planned and orchestrated by film director Zhang Yimou, internationally renowned for his Oscar-nominated epic *Raise the Red Lantern* (1991). To ensure that the ceremony went off without a hitch, 1,000 cloud dispersal rockets had been fired into the air to prevent rain. Security was also at a heightened level to prevent protesters from infiltrating or hijacking the event. Sport played a relatively minor role in the ceremony. Over the next sixteen days, however, China would go on to win 100 medals (51 golds, 21 silvers and 28 bronzes) and thus, for the first time in its history, top the Olympic medals table. Having affirmed its credentials as a major economic and political power on the global stage, the Beijing Games now afforded China an ideal opportunity to display its cultural and sporting might to the world.

Olympic Proliferation

The Beijing Olympics, the 26th time that official summer Games were held in the modern era, certainly established new benchmarks as far as spectacle is concerned. Yet they should also be seen as only the most recent in a long line of Olympic festivals.[3] A further 21 winter Olympic Games, 23 Paralympic Games (summer and winter) and numerous Youth Games, Special Olympics and Deaflympics have also been held throughout the twentieth and twenty-first centuries, a sheer preponderance of activity that gives some indication of how vital a component within international mass culture the Olympic movement has now become. The global expansion of sport in the modern era, both from a participant and spectator perspective, has clearly been a major factor here. Yet, as the opening ceremony at Beijing demonstrated, the Games themselves are, and have always been, far from being simply a sporting festival. Indeed, the visual spectacle of the Games, and the various cultural manifestations that surround them, has always been an integral element not just within the organization and performance of the festivals, but also in the wider dissemination of the Olympics as a mass media event on a global scale.

Interestingly, despite the frequently large crowds in attendance at Olympic stadia, direct spectatorial encounters with the Games might be construed as a relatively rare experience. For example, if the estimated television viewing figures for the Beijing opening ceremony are to be believed, nearly 33,000 spectators witnessed this event via mediated television images for every one spectator in the stadium itself. This, of course, is a far cry from the first Olympic Games of the modern era, held in Athens in 1896 and witnessed predominantly by a local Greek population. Yet even here, both the still camera and newspaper sketch artists were able to produce images of the Games for distribution to a wider community. Indeed, it is precisely this mediated and popularly disseminated nature of visual representations of the Games that is of interest here. Throughout the modern era, the Olympic Games have provided a primary focus for visual culture in its broadest sense. The Games have been photographed and filmed, broadcast through television screens (both domestic and public) and streamed online. They have provided an impetus for paintings, prints and sculptures, for poster, flag, logo and stamp designs, for specially produced artefacts ranging from Olympic medals, torches, mascots and badges and for a whole host of visual ephemera such as cigarette cards and board games. The development of stadium architecture, as well as whole community spaces at Olympic villages, have also been a by-product of the Olympic Games while pageants and theatrical performances have both been inspired by, and integrated into, the Games themselves. Importantly, these various manifestations of visual culture produced within the context of the Games provide vital documentary evidence that serves both to shape our engagement with, and understanding of, the history of the Olympic Games as a global cultural phenomenon.

Visual Legacies

Historians of the modern Olympic Games, like historians of sport more broadly, have perhaps suffered in the past from a near-obsession with list making. Thus the story of the Games has broadly been informed by reams of pages with tables categorizing the names of Olympic victors, runners-up and also-rans, and the nations and institutions they have represented. Olympic narratives are frequently shaped by such statistics; records measured in time, weight or distance achieved, score against an opponent, number of medals secured or competitions participated in; all these are the bread and butter in accounts of past sporting achievement. Individual sports have been documented according to their inclusion in (or exclusion from) the Games while ever-changing rules and regulations determining how these activities will be practiced, have come to form the bedrock of popular understandings of the emergence, development and evolution of the Olympic Games. When historians have reached beyond numerical data to elucidate Olympic history, word-driven accounts have dominated, whether articulated through officially published memoirs, interviews or other forms of oral testimony. All these sources, of course, provide vital documentary evidence that enhances our understanding of how the Games have signified meaning at various historical points. Other forms of evidence, however, can also be accessed and deployed as a useful means to cast light upon past practices and debates. Visual culture, for example, can also provide vital evidence not only of how the Games actually looked at various historical moments, but also how the different modes used for the visual representation of the Games impacted upon how they were interpreted and understood, not least by audiences whose only access to the Games was through this form of visual mediation. To date, however, the deployment of imagery in Olympic histories has tended more towards the casual and the uncritical, frequently appearing as little more than tangential illustrative material to decorate text, and as unworthy of detailed analysis in its own right.[4] This study intends to take a first preliminary step towards redressing this balance by placing visual culture at the very centre of its consideration of Olympic history. Accordingly, the primary focus here will be on the visual, analysing a wide range of cultural artefacts within the context of key moments in the history of the modern Games. The objective is to explore how these cultural artefacts, as vital material traces of history, might enhance, or even transform, our understanding of the ways in which the Games, as a manifestation of mass popular culture, have evolved over the course of just over a century, how they have responded in both imaginative and, at times, controversial ways to the constantly changing socio-historical circumstances of their existence.

The scale of such an undertaking is, of course, both vast and daunting, and inevitably necessitates a high degree of selectivity on the part of the author. Some important activities, such as the Olympic Art competitions held between 1912 and 1948, have been excluded as necessitating full studies in their own right.[5] Other key interventions in visual culture, such as the copious material produced in opposition to the Olympic movement, or works designed and disseminated primarily for regional or specialist, rather than broad international audiences, also play only a minor role here, although this suggests other areas that could yield fascinating results in the future. Rather, emphasis has been placed primarily on key moments, themes and media within the history of the visual representation of the Olympic Games. The sheer plethora of images included in this study certainly reveals both the breadth and diversity of responses to the Games in visual culture. Some inclusions may be extremely well known, for example, Leni Riefenstahl's iconic and infamous cinematic epic, *Olympia* (1936). Others, such as the numerous Olympic posters and, more recently, Olympic mascots may well be visually familiar, even if the names of their producers, and the context of their production, are less so. Famous, and not so famous, Olympians will also make a regular appearance, particularly where their activities have inspired artists, photographers, filmmakers and designers alike. And some images, including documentary photographs of the early Olympic Games, may well be largely unknown, yet I would contend that they provide fascinating insights into the rich and diverse history of the Games. Such an engagement with the visual history of the Olympic Games may well prove to be only a first step in long journey, more a marathon than a sprint. The important task for now is to get off the starting line and into the race.

9

Baron Pierre de Coubertin in Sports Costume, 1883.

one

IMAGING THE ANCIENT OLYMPICS

On 16 June 1894 more than 2,000 guests gathered for a lavish banquet in the amphitheatre at the Sorbonne in Paris. Surrounded by the recently installed Neoclassical mural paintings of Pierre Puvis de Chavannes, they were treated to a performance of 'The Hymn of Apollo', an ancient poem discovered just one year earlier carved in a marble slab at Delphi, now translated into French and set to music composed by no less a figure than Gabriel Fauré.[1] This theatrical spectacle was planned to launch a major international sports conference organized by the French aristocrat Baron Pierre de Coubertin. Among the guests were 79 official delegates from twelve nations, all of whom, over the next eight days, discussed Coubertin's plan to revive the ancient Olympic Games. By the end of what became known as the Sorbonne Congress a new administrative body, the International Olympic Committee (IOC), had been founded and its members had committed to the staging of the first Olympic Games of the modern era in Athens in 1896.[2] Coubertin was unabashed in his strategic use of spectacle as a means both to entice the delegates and a wider public towards support for his plan. 'It seemed to me', he would later write, 'that under the venerable roof of the Sorbonne, the words "Olympic Games" would resound more impressively and persuasively on the audience.'[3] And as Coubertin knew

only too well, the association of his proposed sporting festival with art, poetry and music would certainly help to confer an aura of prestige upon his undertaking. Thus, from its official inception the modern Olympic movement sought to be about far more than just sport. Drawing on the traditions of the ancient Olympic Games other cultural activities were always planned to be an essential element within Olympic festivals, and it was the very fusion of sport and the arts that initially informed Coubertin's perception of Olympism. This notion continued to shape his attitude towards the role that the Olympic Games might play in society right up to his death in 1937 and, to this day, the interconnectedness between sport and the arts is still considered an integral aspect of the Olympic mission.

According to popular Olympic mythology, the concept of reviving the Games of the ancient Greeks first came to Coubertin in a vision. In 1883, at the tender age of just twenty years, the young Coubertin made his first visit across the Channel to study the English educational system. Inspired both by the anglophilia of his compatriot and contemporary Hippolyte Taine, and the literary and nostalgic vision of the English public school as expounded in Thomas Hughes's classic tale of life at Rugby School, *Tom Brown's Schooldays*, Coubertin had developed early a passion for the English emphasis on sport as an integral element within education.[4] Enamoured of the concept of Muscular Christianity, Coubertin valued the athletic chivalry of the English public school system and saw in this a possible antidote to what he perceived to be the physical malaise of his native France, epitomized by the defeat of the nation in the Franco–Prussian War of 1870–71. Throughout much of the rest of his life, Coubertin sought explicitly, though largely unsuccessfully, to encourage a similar principle in the French education system. In 1886, he returned to England to conduct further studies that would lead, in 1888, to his publication *L'Education en Angleterre* (Education in England). On these two trips Coubertin visited many of the nation's best-known public schools, including Eton, Harrow and Winchester, as well as Oxford and Cambridge Universities. It was in the evocative and spiritually inspiring surroundings of the Chapel at Rugby, while standing before the tomb of the school's most famous Headmaster, Dr Thomas Arnold, that he later claimed he was first inspired to undertake his mission to revive the Olympic Games. Over the next decade Coubertin worked tirelessly to bring this vision to fruition. Or so the story goes. Coubertin's account of the origins of the modern Olympic movement can certainly be considered the stuff of legend and continues to shape perceptions of the history of the modern Olympic Games. Yet, as the classicist and Olympic historian David C. Young has claimed, this conventional account charting Coubertin's pivotal role in the revival of the Games has tended to offer an overly simplistic narrative. As Young argues:

> The phrase 'Olympic idea' is usually associated closely, personally, and strongly with Baron Pierre de Coubertin. For many people, it bears great emotional value in that respect, for standard Olympic history credits the baron with being the first to conceive the Olympic revival idea and with achieving it almost single-handedly.[5]

Young does not seek to undermine the importance of the role played by Coubertin. He does, however, posit an alternative pre-history of the Olympic movement in which Coubertin's ideas are less the stuff of visionary inspiration and more derived from the broader pro-Hellenic context of eighteenth- and nineteenth-century European culture. He also places greater emphasis on those individuals whose efforts to bring about a revival of the ancient Olympic Games preceded Coubertin's.

Historical Knowledge of the Ancient Olympics

The original Olympic Games are generally credited as having lasted for over a millennium. First staged around 776 BC, the sporting festival continued to be held at Olympia every four years until its eventual demise, probably by the end of the fourth or beginning of the fifth century.[6] After this, a series of invasions by Visigoths, Avars, Vandals and Slavs contributed to the decimation of the ancient site and by the sixth century, earthquakes and floods had finished the job by burying Olympia beneath several feet of mud and silt. From this point on, Olympia was left relatively undisturbed for over a millennium. Yet despite the disappearance of the actual site, knowledge of the Games had been retained, preserved not least in the copious writings of the ancients, including texts as diverse as the medical treatises of Galen, the histories of Herodotus and Thucydides, the travel accounts of Pausanias and the odes of Pindar.[7] By the time of the Renaissance, a growing passion for

Matthäus Merian, *Olympic Games at the Sanctuary of Zeus in Olympia*, c. 1630, copper engraving.

the Classical era inspired further interest in the Olympic Games and references to the sporting achievements of the ancients began to make an appearance in literary and historical writings. References to the Games also turned up in other cultural forms, notably, for example, in the plays of William Shakespeare. In *Henry VI, Part 3*, for example, George Plantagenet, later Duke of Clarence, looking for a suitable means to inspire his men to battle, specifically invokes the sport of the ancient Greeks when he declares:

> And, if we thrive, promise them such rewards
> As victors wear at the Olympian Games:

This may plant courage in their quailing breasts;
For yet is hope of life and victory.[8]

It was also in England that knowledge of sport in the Classical era led to what has been argued to be the first significant Olympic revival of the modern era; namely the sports and games held annually in a field near Chipping Campden in the Cotswolds, known as Robert Dover's 'Olimpick Games'.

Dover's Games are believed to have their origin in 1612 and were widely referred to as 'Olimpick' at least as early as 1631. They consisted of a variety of events, from traditional English sporting activities such as

13

Illustrated frontispiece representing various activities at Robert Dover's Games, from *Annalia Dubrensia*, 1636.

also included a notable cover illustration. As this represented the various activities that took place during the festival, it can be considered as among the earliest post-Classical visual representations of 'Olimpick' sport. Yet, in visual terms, the illustration notably makes little reference to Classical culture, focusing instead on figures engaging in their activities and dressed in contemporary doublet and hose. This would change dramatically with the emergence of Neoclassicism in the eighteenth century.

Archaeology and the Image of the Games

By the second half of the eighteenth century a fascination not just with history but also with the art and artefacts of the Classical past had come very much to the forefront of intellectual debate. This was much influenced by the ideas of Johann Joachim Winckelmann, whose extolling of the virtues of the 'noble simplicity and quiet grandeur' of the Hellenistic era proved highly influential and contributed towards the birth of both art history and archaeology as disciplines.[10] From his earliest days, Winckelmann was virtually obsessed with Olympia and even claimed that in his youth he had dreamt of being transported to the site of the ancient Games and there encountered the splendours of classical antiquity in their original setting. In 1766, when Winckelmann became aware of British archaeologist Richard Chandler's re-discovery of Olympia, he began to plan a trip to the ancient site of the Games. Sadly his untimely death just two years later prevented this from materializing. Chandler's find soon attracted widespread interest regarding both Olympia and the history of the Games, although it would be another 63 years before archaeological work would begin and well over a century before the German Professor Ernst Curtius

hunting, coursing and horse racing, to dancing, musical performances and card and board games. Various running and throwing competitions were also included in the programme. Little documented at the time, these Games are best known today from a surviving pamphlet published in 1636. Diminutive both in scale and number of copies produced, the *Annalia Dubrensia* (The Annals of Dover) includes 33 poems, some by well-known poets of the day (Michael Drayton, Ben Jonson, Thomas Heywood), many of which draw explicit parallels between the ancient Olympic Games and Dover's festival. As just one example among many, William Durham thus claimed that Dover's 'Olimpicks' did no less than 'bring Arcadia to our Cotswold Hills'.[9] Intriguingly, the *Annalia Dubrensia*

Columns in the Olympic Gymnasium.

would undertake the extensive archaeological project that brought detailed knowledge of Olympia's history to light.[11]

Even while Olympia lay unexplored, however, other archaeological finds began to contribute towards building up not just historical knowledge, but specifically a visual image of the ancient Games. Fragments of Greek pots were regularly uncovered during the eighteenth and nineteenth centuries and were increasingly collected and catalogued. Here the formation of the great public museums throughout Europe, most notably the British Museum in London and the Museé de Louvre in Paris, facilitated the systematic study and display of these artefacts as well as bringing them to the attention of a wider public.

Sport, particularly the Olympic Games, had proven a popular subject for Greek craftsmen and thus the surviving fragments of these often exquisitely decorated objects enabled scholars to build up a more detailed vision of ancient athletes. These representations, frequently depicting competitors at various stages of their sporting endeavours, thus enhanced existing knowledge of the Games and acted as a catalyst to draw the interest of those who linked modern sporting developments to those of the past. The discovery of famous antique works – most notably Myron's *Discobolus* and Polykleitos' *Diadoumenos* (athlete binding a victory fillet around his head) – contributed further both to the factual knowledge and heroic status of the ancient Games.

15

Panathenaic prize amphora, signed by the potter Kittos, c. 367–366 BC.

A long-jumper and a discus-thrower in an Etruscan wall painting from c. 520 BC.

Discobolus, Roman marble copy of a bronze original of the 5th century BC by Myron; from Hadrian's Villa near Rome.

James Barry, detail from 'Crowning the Victors at Olympia', from the cycle *The Progress of Human Knowledge and Culture*, 1777–84, oil on canvas.

Knowledge of these classical prototypes also contributed towards contemporary artists beginning to engage with the ancient Olympic Games as a subject for their own works. To take one example, the British history painter James Barry notably included a scene entitled *Crowning the Victors at Olympia* in his vast series of murals representing *The Progress of Human Knowledge and Culture*, produced for the Great Room at the Royal Society of Arts in London between 1777 and 1784. Throughout the nineteenth century, sculptors, too, frequently drew upon these famous representations of ancient Greek athletes as a precedent for their own work. In both France and Britain, for example, the latter part of the nineteenth century witnessed a growing interest in the development of new sculptural forms that not only emphasized the corporeal nature of the nude male athlete in action, but also frequently made an explicit reference to the

Heinrich Leutemann, *Olympic Games: Four-horse Carriage Racing in the Hippodrome*, c. 1865, woodcut.

William Blake Richmond, *An Athlete*, 1879, bronze; in St Peter's Square, Hammersmith, London.

preponderance of representations of Olympian athletes in Classical Greek sculpture. These works, it might be added, not only reflected knowledge of the ancient Games, they also notably appeared at precisely the time when attempts were being made to revive the Games for a new generation.

Reviving the Games: From Zappas and Brookes to Coubertin

Here it is important to recognize that the revival of the Olympic Games in the late nineteenth century had its roots as much in this wider historical, cultural and visual context than Coubertin's notional moment of divine inspiration might suggest. Coubertin was very much a child of his era and his fascination with the ancient Olympic Games was thus informed by the socio-cultural milieu in which he lived. As Young notes, however, Coubertin's ambition to revive the Olympic Games for a modern era also drew upon the direct activities of those who had come before him. Young was not the first scholar to examine this pre-history of the modern Olympic movement; key sport historians including Richard D. Mandell, John MacAloon and Joachim Rühl had already trodden this path in the 1970s and '80s.[12] However, Young's study does shift the focus toward the ideas and activities of other earlier nineteenth-century individuals who had previously been sidelined in Olympic histories. These include two Greeks, the poet Panagiotis Soutsos and the businessman Evangelis Zappas, and an Englishman, Dr William Penny Brookes.

For Young, the origin of the modern Olympic movement 'seems to have begun as the glancing thought of a poet'.[13] In 1833, just one year after the newly independent Greek state had crowned its first monarch of the modern era, Soutsos published a

poem entitled 'Dialogue of the Dead'. The work is not untypical of romantic poetry of the period, not least in looking to a classical past as a source of inspiration for modern Greece. As part of his dialogue Soutsos, like Coubertin after him, also invokes a vision, here the ghost of Plato who bemoans the state of modern Greece compared to the glories of its ancient past. In a now much quoted extract from the poem, Plato poses the rhetorical question: 'Where are your Olympic Games? . . . Your great festivals, your great theatres, the marble statues, where are they?'[14] It is important to note here, as Young points out, that even within this early evocation of Olympic revivalism, sport within the Olympic Games is seen as but one component within a much wider cultural enterprise. For Soutsos, music, literature and art are as much a part of the Olympic ideal as sport, and all are in need of revival if Greece is to become great once more. Within two years of publishing 'Dialogue of the Dead', Soutsos's poetic conceit was transformed into a more literal question when he approached the Greek government with a detailed proposal to revive the Olympic Games in Greece.[15] Despite the approval of the newly crowned monarch, King Otto, it would be another two decades before plans to stage the first Greek Olympics of the modern era would be developed, and it was at this point that Zappas entered the stage.

By the mid-1850s Zappas had amassed a vast fortune and, like Soutsos, wished to restore the Greece of his ancestors to its former glory.[16] In 1856 he wrote to the Greek king and offered to finance, in its entirety, a revival of the Olympic Games, thus effectively bankrolling Soutsos's initial proposal. Three years later, this came to fruition when the city of Athens staged a host of athletic events including foot races, throwing events and jumping competitions, all under the banner of 'Olympic Games'. To promote the modernity of the

Greek nation, an industrial exhibition was also staged as part of the broader Olympic programme, and a grand opening ceremony was held to add to the splendour of the occasion. Although the original proposal was to hold these Games every four years, the second staging was delayed until 1870, five years after Zappas's death. A combination of governmental paralysis and legal wrangling over Zappas's legacy contributed to this delay. In 1875 the third Zappas Games took place, although entry to the various competitions was restricted to the so-called more 'cultured' classes.[17] The Games were widely reported as a failure. In 1888 a fourth event was held but, unfortunately, the sporting events were cancelled. A fifth proposed staging of the Zappas Olympics, planned for 1892, was also eventually cancelled.

While Zappas's revival of the Olympic Games was experiencing a rise and fall in Greece, back in England the activities of William Penny Brookes were also putting the Olympics back on the map. Both a medic and a philanthropist in the Victorian tradition, Brookes sought to improve conditions for the working class in his native village of Much Wenlock in Shropshire. To this end, in 1840 he established a reading society for the use of the local working community. Ten years later his interests in social improvement extended to physical activity when he founded what was to be known as the Wenlock Olympian Class. A key objective of this society was to hold annual games to encourage outdoor physical activities and to include athletic events, team games and traditional country sports. Like Zappas, Brookes derived much from contemporary knowledge of the ancient Olympic festivals. Thus his Games commenced with a procession, headed by a herald, and events included individual running, jumping and throwing competitions. Laurel crowns were also awarded to victors

Hunt & Roskell, design for the pentathlon medal awarded at the Wenlock Olympian Games, 1865–6, silver.

and, in a clear homage to the ancient Games, a pentathlon was introduced in 1868, though with some variation in the five contests that formed the original pentathlon at Olympia.[18] Brookes clearly regarded the pentathlon as a major component within the Wenlock Olympian programme, as evidenced by the special silver medal he had designed as a prize for the winner. This, too, made explicit reference to the ancient Olympics both in its representation of Nike, the Goddess of Victory, surrounded by a crown of olive leaves and its inscription 'there are rewards for glorious deeds', a line taken from one of Pindar's Olympic Odes. The medal, designed by Hunt &

Charles Ainsworth, Champion Tilter, Being Crowned with Olive Leaves at the Wenlock Olympian Games, 1887.

Roskell, silversmiths to Queen Victoria, also reflects Brookes's emphasis on cultural activities beyond just sport. Thus the bar from which the medallion itself is suspended includes four shields representing literature, music, sculpture and painting, as well as sport. Military skills are also notably represented in these shields.

Though clearly inspired by the passion for all things Greek that characterized much Victorian culture, the Wenlock Games developed into more than a simple allusion to the classical past. Indeed Brookes was also interested in reviving and reinventing traditional English pastimes. Thus, in 1858, he introduced 'tilting at the ring' into the annual programme, an event that featured equestrian lancers seeking to spear a metal ring while galloping at full speed. This explicit reference to jousting thus added a medieval dimension to the Games. Yet Brookes was only too happy to mix and match such references, as is made evident in a photograph showing the prize-giving ceremony for the tilting competition in 1887. Here, the champion,

Charles Ainsworth, is seen kneeling before a young, female dignitary who offers her 'favour' for his victory. The prize, however, is not a personal possession of the lady, but the laurel crown so resonant of ancient Olympia.

While Brookes certainly emphasized a historicist element within his Games, he did not eschew modern technology entirely. In 1876, for example, a three-mile cycling race was introduced into the proceedings, notably at a time when the nearby cities of Birmingham and Coventry were world leaders in the manufacture of bicycles. At this time the so-called high-wheel bicycle, popularly known as the penny-farthing, was at the cutting edge of bicycle technology and constituted the fastest form of human-powered locomotion. As such, it was widely embraced by young, male, Victorian thrill seekers and became one of the first forms of racing bicycle in the history of the sport. Sadly, no contemporary images representing the Wenlock Olympian bicycle race are known to exist. However, a portrait of the first winner of the event, Thomas Sabin, can be found in the archive of the Wenlock Olympian Society. The image displays many of the conventions of Victorian photographic portraiture. Thus Sabin is represented in an indoor studio setting before a landscape backdrop framed by trees and hollyhocks. He is dressed in a sports vest and shorts, to confirm his status as sportsman, yet his hair is carefully coiffured and he adopts a somewhat formal pose with left hand on hip. The bulk of the image, however, is taken up by his sporting equipment; the penny-farthing bicycle upon which he proudly leans in acknowledgement of the vital link between man and machine that has brought about his success. Notably, both athlete and bicycle are placed in close proximity to a stunted tree trunk positioned in front of the backdrop. Incongruous in a narrative sense, this prop is included specifically to recall the use of such devices in marble statues of athletes, such as the Roman copies after Myron and Polykleitos, thus lending Sabin a certain classical air, despite the intrinsic modernity of his sporting practice.

In 1860, no doubt influenced by the first staging of Zappas's Games in Athens, Brookes extended his local event into a countywide competition. Much Wenlock thus played host to the inaugural Shropshire Olympian Games, with plans put in place to hold this annual event at different towns throughout the county in subsequent years. By now, Brookes's activities were leaving their mark elsewhere in Britain. In 1862, the Olympic revivalism bug had spread to Liverpool, which that year had witnessed the first Liverpool Olympics, held at Mount Vernon Parade Grounds. In stark contrast to Brookes's philanthropic agenda, however, the organizers of this event, John Hulley and Charles Melly, sought to exclude the working class from competing by drawing up a strict amateur code, thus for the first time invoking the amateur-professional divisions that

Thomas Sabin of Coventry, Winner of the Three-mile Bicycle Race in 1877 and 1878.

would plague Olympic history up to the end of the twentieth century. The gentleman-amateur Liverpool Games proved a great success and were restaged both in 1863 and 1864. In 1865, a Grand Olympian Festival was held in North Wales at Llandudno. By now, Hulley had joined forces with Brookes to establish the National Olympic Association (NOA) and together they planned to hold the biggest Olympic event to date, a National Olympic Games in London. Regional jealousies and concerns over the potential participation of

Postcard illustrating crowds at the Panathenaic stadium in Athens during the inaugural Olympic Games in 1896.

two

THE BIRTH OF THE MODERN OLYMPIC GAMES

Less than two years after the closing speeches at the Sorbonne Congress, over 240 athletes from fourteen nations gathered in Athens to participate in the inaugural Olympic Games of the modern era. Consistent with Coubertin's earlier ideas, pageantry and spectacle were to play a major part long before any sporting activity took place. For example, on the eve of the Games, Easter Sunday, a large crowd gathered to attend the unveiling of a monument to Georgios Averoff, the Greek philanthropist whose generosity had enabled the restoration of the Panathenaic stadium. Originally built by Herodes Atticus in the first century AD, the stadium had been home to the ancient Panathenaic Games and would now host most of the sporting competitions at the modern event. As was evident to many of the organizers, Averoff's financial support had not only provided the city with a beautifully restored building, but had also been instrumental in ensuring that the Games took place at all. It was thus hardly surprising that the property tycoon was so honoured. Yet the erection of this statue, financed by public subscription and produced by the Greek nation's most respected sculptor, Georgios Vroutos, was more than just a gesture of appreciation to a kindly benefactor. Placed directly in front of the entrance to the stadium, where it stands to this day, and carved from the same Pentelic marble used in the reconstruction of the stadium, the Averoff monument was an explicit gesture of Greek national pride. The ceremony was presided over by the Greek royal family and marching bands and speeches accompanied the unveiling, as a Greek national flag was unfurled to reveal the figure of a proud Averoff proffering a gesture of welcome to the athletes and spectators of the world. The Averoff monument became a key focal point for the official opening of the Games the next day, notably the anniversary of Greek independence, and subsequently for the whole event. Here, the message was loud and clear. Greece had been the historical home of the ancient Olympic Games. Now, it was also to be the spiritual home to the modern Olympic Games. The nationalist competitiveness that would subsequently shape much Olympic history was thus established even before the Games themselves had begun.

Evidence documenting these first Olympic Games can be drawn from a number of textual sources. These include contemporary press reports, accounts written by competitors, spectators and other eyewitnesses, and the lavishly produced Official Report of the Olympic Games. The visual evidence for the Games, however, is less extensive. As cinema was still in its infancy, no movie footage of the Games is known to exist and relatively few press photographers regarded

Georgios Vroutos, *Georgios Averoff*, erected outside the newly restored Panathenaic stadium in Athens, 1896, marble.

The Inaugural Games as Viewed Through the Filter of the Popular Illustrated Magazine: Castaigne and Linson

In April 1896, the American illustrated monthly magazine *The Century* offered its readers a brief history of the Olympics in an article entitled 'The Old Olympic Games'. The article was accompanied by ten illustrations by André Castaigne, featuring scenes representing runners, the chariot race, the Hoplite race (racing in armour) and the Pankration (a form of no-holds-barred wrestling). The article also included multiple scenes of the victory parade and ceremonies that concluded the ancient festival. Castaigne was a highly suitable artist to fulfil this commission. Having studied painting under Jean-Léon Gérôme at the Ecole des Beaux-Arts in Paris, he was well versed in history painting and familiar with the passion for all things Greek that character-ized much late nineteenth-century European art production. *The Century*'s focus on the ancient Olympics was clearly intended to coincide with the revived Games in Athens, which were also highlighted in an editorial under the broad title 'Topics of the Time'. Here, the journal bemoaned the paucity of American competitors participating, a consequence, it claimed, of 'the distance and the unwonted season'.[1] Despite these obstacles, however, *The Century* declared its patriotic commit-ment to the modern Olympic movement by proudly announcing that it would later be publishing an article on the Games penned by no less than the Baron Pierre de Coubertin himself. It was with equal pride that it informed its readers that it had sent its own in-house illustrator, Castaigne, to document the event. Castaigne's illustrations, along with Coubertin's article, subsequently appeared in the November issue of the journal.

these first Olympics as worthy of coverage. However, among the reporters who did travel to Athens, three notably documented their experiences in visual form. These include the French-born artist and printmaker, André Castaigne, the American illustrator, Corwin Knapp Linson, and the German photographer, Albert Meyer. And it is thanks to the work of these individuals that a visual record of the first Olympic Games of the modern era remains available today.

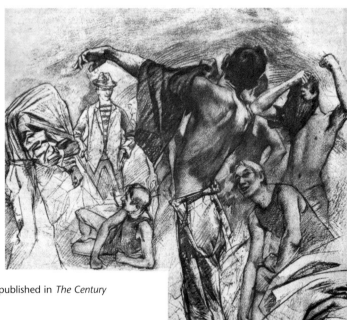

André Castaigne, 'One of Our Boys', illustration published in *The Century* (November 1896).

André Castaigne, 'Athletes Preparing for Competition', another illustration published in *The Century* (November 1896).

Covering a sporting event was clearly a new departure for Castaigne and proved something of a challenge. Indeed it is noteworthy that only two of his nine illustrations specifically represented sporting action. The first of these focused on the fencing event held at the Zappeion in Athens, the second on the end of the marathon race. Even in this latter image sport plays second fiddle as the tiny runner seen in the distance is dwarfed by the exotically dressed and exuberant foreground spectators. Instead, Castaigne represented groups of athletes in preparation for competition, the large crowds at the Panathenaic stadium and the festivals and ceremonies that accompanied the Games. In a gesture of patriotic fervour probably directed towards the readers of *The Century*, he also included an illustration of an anonymous American athlete standing proudly to attention at the entrance to the stadium, holding the furled flag of the United States in his right hand. Thus Castaigne

notably emphasized not only the presence of American athletes at the inaugural Games, but also their victories for, despite sending only a limited number of competitors, the United States won more events than any other nation.[2] In this context, Castaigne's visual celebration of the unknown American athlete might be read as a retort to the Averoff national monument, challenging the Greek nation's statement of ownership of all things Olympic and making an explicit claim for the more internationalist nature of the Games.

The Century was not the only illustrated journal to cover the Athens Games. Its competitor *Scribner's Magazine* also highlighted the ancient Olympics in its

April 1896 issue, publishing a short story by Duffield Osborne recounting the exploits of the fictive Phraanes the Mede during his first visit to the Games.[3] The story was illustrated with drawings by the magazine's regular contributor, Corwin Knapp Linson. To reinforce its interest in the current Games, the same issue also included a report on the restoration of the Panathenaic Stadium, written by the scholar and director of the American School of Classical Studies in Athens, Rufus B. Richardson.[4] As an American living in Athens, Richardson was also recruited by *Scribner's Magazine* to report on the revived Games and, in September 1896, published an article under the title 'The New Olympian Games'.[5] Accompanying Richardson's text were 20 drawings by Linson who, like Castaigne, had been sent to Athens to produce a visual record of this ground-breaking event.

Adopting a similar approach to Castaigne, Linson placed a great deal of emphasis on the pomp and

Corwin Knapp Linson, 'The Greek Discus Thrower Sotirios Versis', published in *Scribner's Magazine* (September 1896).

THE FINISH OF THE HURDLE RACE.
(Marathon Day.)

urtis, the American, leading; Goulding, the Englishman, a close second.

Corwin Knapp Linson, 'The Finish of the Hurdle Race', illustration published in *Scribner's Magazine* (September 1896).

ceremony attached to the Games, as evidenced by his many illustrations of crowds at the stadium, the victory celebrations and nocturnal festivals. Unlike his contemporary, however, Linson paid more attention to the sporting events, producing several illustrations of individual athletes in action. Hurdlers, shot-putters, long-jumpers, wrestlers, fencers and discus-throwers all made an appearance in Linson's work, many explicitly identified by name in the hand-written or printed captions. Perhaps inevitably, given his designated audience, Linson focused predominantly on victorious American athletes. Thus James Connolly (winner of the first modern Olympic medal for triple-jump), Thomas Curtis (winner of the 110-metre hurdles) and Robert Garrett (winner of the shot-put and discus competitions) were all represented on the pages of Richardson's article. Indeed, only one non-American athlete can be identified in Linson's illustrations: the defeated Greek discus-thrower Sotirios Versis. Even here, identification is dependent upon the handwritten inscription in Greek text.

For both Castaigne and Linson, visually documenting the events of 1896 tested the very limits of their ability, not least because few pictorial conventions existed for the representation of sport. Castaigne's solution to this problem was largely to avoid sporting action, focusing instead on representations of athletes adopting poses not dissimilar to those of the

Corwin Knapp Linson, 'The Discus, Just Before the Throw', published in *Scribner's Magazine* (September 1896).

life-drawing classes that formed part of his education. Linson took a more courageous stance, attempting to capture athletes in motion, as evidenced by his images of hurdlers and long-jumpers. It must be acknowledged, however, that these images are rather stilted and awkward. Linson's drawing style was less than suitable for an emphasis on the frozen sporting moment and thus the images fail to capture the energy and excitement as articulated in the accompanying texts. Far more engaging, however, are Linson's representations of discus-throwers, depicted at the precise moment before they start their swing. These images, clearly derived from precedents in classical sculpture such as Myron's *Discobolus*, perhaps capture more successfully the harmonious combination of mental concentration and physical strength required of athletes at the peak of their performance.

Albert Meyer and the First Olympic Photographs

In addition to the illustrators, Castaigne and Linson, a third professional artist also made the arduous journey to Athens in 1896. Albert Meyer had already established his reputation as a photographer in Berlin by the early 1890s. Shortly before the Games were due to commence, he was introduced to Willibald Gebhardt, the man responsible for ensuring Germany's participation in the revived Olympics. Recognizing a commercial opportunity, Meyer agreed to accompany Gebhardt and the German athletes on the trip to Athens and thus became one of only a handful of photographers to document the first Games of the modern era.[6] It is unknown precisely how many photographs Meyer took, but seventeen of his images were subsequently reproduced in the Official Report compiled for the IOC. A similar number was published in the German sports

Engraving from *Le Petit Journal* of the French cyclist Paul Masson, gold medallist at the 1896 Athens Olympic Games.

and even the production of commemorative stamps illustrated with examples of Greek classical sculpture representing ancient sports. The ceremonial awarding of olive branches to victors at a grand closing ceremony also served to reinforce this reference to the ancient Games. Yet at no point did the new event seek to avoid the intrusion of modernity. Unlike its classical precedent, the modern Olympics eschewed the Pan-Hellenic emphasis of the ancient Games, instead inviting athletes from all nations to compete. Nor, perhaps thankfully, did athletes compete naked as had been the convention in the ancient Olympics since 720 BC.[12] Further, modern events not practiced at the ancient Olympics, such as shooting, cycling, swimming, tennis and gymnastics were all introduced into the new Games. In a lighter vein, this conflation of modernity and Classicism was aptly caricatured in the English satirical magazine *Punch*, which included

'The Revival of the Olympic Games at Athens: Portion of a Design for the Suggested Restoration of the Frieze of the Parthenon in Commemoration of the Event', published in *Punch* (April 1896).

THE REVIVAL OF THE OLYMPIC GAMES AT ATHENS.

Portion of a Design for the suggested restoration of the Frieze of the Parthenon in commemoration of the event.

a proposed 'Design for the Suggested Restoration of the Frieze of the Parthenon' in commemoration of the staging of the Games of 1896.

The Invention of the Marathon

Perhaps the most notable example of an attempt to fuse modernity and tradition at the Athens Games was the staging of the marathon race. Long-distance foot races had not, in fact, been a feature of the ancient Olympic Games. Indeed, the longest recorded event was the *dolichos*, a race of approximately 4 kilometres. The inaugural Olympic marathon would be contested over a course ten times that distance. The idea for the race was very much a modern concoction, usually credited to the French philologist Michel Bréal. Run over the distance between Marathon and Athens, the new race notionally referenced a same run undertaken by Pheidippides (or Eukles) in *c.* 490 BC to bring news of Athenian victory over the Persians. Yet this tale was broadly known to be historically dubious. In fact it was an amalgamation of many historical references from Herodotus to Plutarch. Nonetheless, aware of the popularly perceived classical resonance

of such a run, Bréal proposed to Coubertin that the race be introduced as the climax of the athletic events, a novel spectacle to attract both public and press attention. Certainly the significance of the marathon was enhanced not only by Bréal's gift of a specially made silver cup, but the additional donation of an antique Greek vase representing a scene from the ancient Games, both prizes to be awarded to the victor. What could not have been predicted at this point, however, was the historical resonance that the race would take on as a consequence of the result. When the contest commenced, on the fifth day of competition, Greek athletes were yet to record a victory in the track and field competitions. As thirteen of the seventeen marathon competitors were Greek, chances of a home victory appeared strong. Yet despite these hopes the four non-Greeks – Albin Lermusiaux (France), Edwin Flack (Australia), Arthur Blake (United States) and Gyula Kellner (Hungary) – dominated the field for much of the race. As the competitors approached the end, however, these athletes gradually faded to be overtaken by the eventual winner and hero of the hour, the Greek runner, Spiridon Louis. Fellow Greek runners also finished in second and third place, thus resulting in a clean sweep for the home nation.

Before Louis had recaptured his breath, his victory was already acquiring mythological status. Having secured a home victory in an event purposely designed to recall the glories of Greece's classical past, Louis was instantly fêted as a national hero. According to various reports, he was offered countless prizes in honour of his victory for the nation, ranging from the gift of a watch from an admiring lady, to free meals for a year and the free services of a barber for the rest of his life.[13] In one of the more bizarre myths emanating from this saga, a wealthy young woman allegedly offered her hand in marriage to the victor in the marathon race, expecting this to be one of the aristocratic young men competing, rather than Louis, a mere water-carrier from a poor farming family. The resilience of this doubtless apocryphal tale may be judged by the fact that it formed the basis for a Hollywood comedy starring Jayne Mansfield, released in 1962 under the title *It Happened in Athens*.

While stories in the popular press certainly fuelled the growing Louis mythology, the role of Castaigne, Linson and Meyer should not be entirely overlooked. Indeed, all three notably focused their attention on the victorious Greek athlete. Linson, perhaps, paid the least attention of the three to Louis's victory, though it is noteworthy that his *Presentation of Prizes* places the Greek athlete at the centre of the composition. Instantly recognizable by his traditional costume, Louis is here the focal point not only for the spectator of Linson's work, but also for the various dignitaries and the vast audience of spectators represented within the image. Castaigne, on the other hand, was clearly more captivated by the exotic appearance of Louis. While Louis, the athlete, appears as a mere distant speck in his illustration *Arrival of the Winner of the*

André Castaigne, 'The Parade of the Winners', published in *The Century* (November 1896).

Marathon Race, Louis, in traditional Greek costume, makes a more prominent appearance in *The King Presenting the Awards* and *The Parade of the Winners*. Thus the Greek marathon victor appears in three of the nine illustrations produced by Castaigne for *The Century*. Meyer, too, clearly recognized the visual potency of Louis dressed in his traditional Greek costume. Of the twenty or so sporting portraits produced by Meyer at the Games, only the one that represents Louis departs from posing the subject in athletic costume. Indeed, in the absence of contextual knowledge, nothing in Meyer's photograph of Louis would betray his status as sportsman and Olympic

Albert Meyer, *Spyridon Louis, Winner of the Marathon at the Inaugural Olympic Games in Athens*, 1896.

victor. His proud stance, with right hand on hip, and confident gaze directly at the spectator rather suggest the assurance and pride of a national type, more than that of an individual, thus reflecting the degree to which Louis's personal achievement was already being registered as symptomatic of a revival of Greek national prowess. Castaigne, Linson and Meyer thus all concurred in their individual representations of Louis not as a sporting, but rather as a national, victor. Accordingly, this image of Louis was widely disseminated, published in the Official Report, the popular illustrated press across the Atlantic, the photographic albums of Meyer, sent as gifts to many

of the crowned heads of Europe, and in the German illustrated sports press. All this served to confirm Louis's status as the pre-eminent personality of the Games in 1896, and as a symbol for Greek nationhood. While the home nation may not have secured the most victories in the Athens Games, the image of Spiridon Louis certainly ensured that it gained the most widespread media coverage.

From Athens to Paris

When plans to revive the Olympic Games were first announced in 1894, it was agreed not only that Athens would host the first event, but also that, thereafter, subsequent Olympic festivals Games would be held at other international venues on a roving basis. Further, the Congress approved Paris as the host city for the proposed Games in 1900. However, the outstanding success of events in Athens jeopardized these plans. The Greek authorities certainly valued the international prestige afforded the nation as a consequence of staging the Games and immediately adopted a proposal, purportedly made by the British Prince of Wales, that Athens now be made permanent home to the modern Olympics. Other participating nations, enamoured of the classical resonances conferred on the Games by the Greek setting, concurred with this view, not least the entire American team who signed a memorandum expressing their view that 'these Games should never be moved from their native soil'.[14] As Greek euphoria began to diminish, however, Coubertin's personal determination to follow through with his original plan became more entrenched and the likelihood of Athens retaining the Olympic Games quickly faded. Plans for the 1900 Paris Games began to be forged.

The Games of 1900 have frequently been described as the forgotten Olympics.[15] Though originally intended

Poster for an international fencing competition, Paris, 1900.

as a second manifestation of Coubertin's golden-age sporting festival brought to the French capital, the Games ended up as something of a damp squib. Seeking to benefit from the broad publicity that accompanied the government-sponsored Exposition Universelle of 1900, the IOC agreed to link the Games with this major event, thus relinquishing control to the French state. However, as the Exposition was planned as a celebration of modernity, technology and science, Coubertin's passion for Classicism was largely seen as an anachronism, not least by the Exposition's chief organizer, Alfred Picard. Accordingly, associations with the classical past were swiftly suppressed and the Paris Games ended up bearing little resemblance to the precedent established in Athens. In contrast to the original sharply focused and self-contained event, framed by an opening and closing ceremony and held over a period of less than a fortnight, the sporting competitions in Paris took place sporadically and stretched out over the entire six-month duration of the Exposition. Furthermore, over 58,000 competitors took part in the various competitions, in contrast to the approximate 240 at Athens, while a host of one-off competitions not subsequently associated with the Olympics, including angling, ballooning, kite flying and pigeon racing, were included in the programme. No official medals were awarded and open cash prizes were offered to professional competitors, again in contrast to the amateur ethos of the Athens Games. Most damaging of all, however, was the fact that the organizers of the Exposition Universelle did not even allow the designation 'Olympic' to be used. Thus the competitions were publicized simply as *concours internationaux* (international competitions). As a consequence of this, the extent to which many of the sporting events held at the Paris Games of 1900 can be designated 'Olympic' has courted much controversy.[16]

Given the fragmentary nature of the Paris Games, relatively little visual evidence has been preserved. What remains consists predominantly of amateur photographs produced by spectators or competitors. Even the near 800-page Official Report carried only a handful of photographs taken during competition, and these are confined exclusively to the ballooning and diving competitions. The Report did, however, include one important set of images, which might be seen as reflecting the notable change of emphasis from the past to the present, from the classical to the scientific, that characterized events at the 1900 Paris Olympics.

Marey and the Science of Sporting Movement

One of the little-known achievements of the 1900 Games was a scientific study carried out by a team of researchers under the leadership of the physiologist Étienne-Jules Marey. Better known today as a pioneer photographer, Marey had established his position as Professor of Physiology at the Collège de France by the late 1860s. His interests in photography only emerged later when he saw the medium as an ideal tool to facilitate and enhance his analysis of animal and human locomotion. By the 1880s Marey had developed a technique known as chronophotography – the production of multiple images captured at high-speed which thus rendered the movement of animate beings easily legible. At this time, he combined forces with the physical culturist Georges Demeny to produce a series of photographic studies of gymnasts in motion. Marey and Demeny, like Coubertin, were inspired by widespread concerns regarding the potential physical degeneracy of the French citizen since defeat in the Franco–Prussian War of 1870–71. Thus they sought

Étienne-Jules Marey, *Richard Sheldon, Gold Medallist at the 1900 Olympic Games in Paris, Putting the Shot*, photograph reproduced in *Concours internationaux d'exercises physiques et de sports*, vol. II (1900).

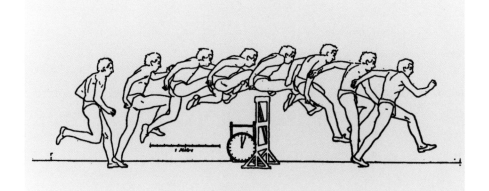

Étienne-Jules Marey, *Sketch of the American athlete Alvin Kraenzlein Jumping a Hurdle*, reproduced in *Concours internationaux d'exercises physiques et de sports*, vol. II (1900).

Photo finish of the 100-metres dash at the 1948 London Olympic Games.

to analyse the current physical condition of the nation by studying the images they produced. These, they argued, would provide a sound, scientific basis upon which to develop new methods for the physical improvement of the nation.[17] With the staging of the Games in Paris, Marey now saw an ideal opportunity to examine the world's best athletes in action.

In the Official Report, Marey declared that the explicit objective of his project was 'to study the effects of different sports on the body and to compare their impacts upon health'.[18] However, the visual evidence he gathered suggests a wider objective; namely, to acquire detailed images that documented the physical movements of the best American athletes as a means to improve the performances of his fellow countrymen. Marey originally attempted to photograph athletes in

the field, but found the extraneous detail of crowd, shadow and background too intrusive. Thus he asked some of the competitors to replicate their practices in his specially designed studio in the Bois de Boulogne. Here, Marey photographed the precise movements of the American hurdler Alvin Kraenzlein (winner of the 60 metres, 110-metre hurdles, and 200-metre hurdles races and the long jump), Richard Sheldon (winner of the shot-put) and high-jump world record-holder, Mike Sweeney. From these photographs, Marey reconstructed drawings that highlighted the successful techniques adopted by the Americans, thus providing a visual blueprint for athletic trainers who could now analyse the movements of the most successful competitors and thus assist their own athletes in replicating these. Marey's visual research at the Games of 1900 can thus be seen as

41

instrumental in the emergence and expansion of sports science, not least the deployment of the photographic medium to enable detailed study of physical performance, or to establish the final position of competitors in close-run finishes. At the same time, a comparison of Marey's photographs of Olympic athletes with, say, Meyer's representation of Garrett, gives a good indication of the extent to which the emphasis on science and technology at the Paris Games of 1900 had already eclipsed the nostalgic Classicism of Athens 1896.

Meet Me in St Louis . . . or back in Athens?

The Paris Games were widely perceived as a pale shadow after the success of Athens. Incorporating the event into the Exposition Internationale served only to dilute the impact of the Games while the absence of virtually every reference to Olympic origins seriously diminished their significance. Yet even in the wake of this fiasco, it appears that Coubertin and the IOC learned very little. In 1901 it was announced that the Games of the third Olympiad would be held in Chicago, thus bringing the Games to the New World. Soon, however, it became evident that Chicago's interest was waning in favour of the city of St Louis, Missouri, which was scheduled to hold a major World's Fair in 1904 to celebrate the centenary of the Louisiana Purchase.[19] Thus the Games of 1904, though this time at least designated as Olympic, would once more be incorporated within a bigger event and held over an extended period of time. The sheer distance between mainland Europe and the American Midwest was also to prove something of a problem as this precluded the involvement of many international athletes. Indeed, fewer than 10 per cent of the competitors at the St Louis Games came from outside the United States and Canada

while over 85 per cent of the medals awarded went to the United States. The shameful events of the 'Anthropology Days' (discussed in more detail in chapter Six), during which so-called 'primitive' peoples were asked to compete in Western sports with the sole objective of proving the 'superiority' of the white race, shocked many and cast a further pall over events. By the end of 1904, the Olympic revival movement was virtually in disarray. Of the three Games held to date, Athens alone could be regarded as anything approaching a success. And it was Athens that now stood up to save the reputation of the IOC.

Following the Greek attempt in 1896 to establish Athens as the permanent home to the Olympic Games, a second proposal was put forward to introduce so-called Intercalary Games. These were to be held in Athens at the mid-point between the official Olympic festivals. Throughout the next decade Coubertin and the IOC opposed this proposal but, after the second debacle in St Louis, reluctantly agreed to stage such an event in 1906. Olympic history has not been kind to the Athens Games of 1906. The results from these Games are still excluded from official recognition and, when this event is included in IOC publications, it is usually given only the briefest of consideration.[20] Yet the 1906 Athens Games may well have saved the Olympic movement from an ignominious demise. Once again, all eyes were focused on a single sporting festival with a host of international participants, confined to a period of just over a week. Planning and organization seem to have been exemplary and many Olympic traditions – including the flag march around the stadium for the opening ceremony – were introduced for the first time.[21] The return to the Greek capital also allowed the classical resonances that had largely been excluded from the previous two Games to emerge once more, as is made evident by the inclusion

Weightlifter Dimitrios Tofalos at the 10th anniversary of the revival of the Olympic Games, Athens, 1906.

of an image of Myron's *Discobolus* on the cover of a special edition of *Spalding's Athletic Library*, published in New York to celebrate the Games. Much as Olympia was the home of the ancient Games, Athens has some right to claim its status not only as the birthplace of the modern Games, but also as a sustaining centre during this first decade of the Olympic revival. Yet despite the strong links forged between the ancient and modern sporting worlds in the Panathenaic stadium in both

1896 and 1906, it would be the best part of another century before the Olympic Games would return, once more, to the land of their forefathers. It is perhaps a fitting tribute, however, that the image of the Panathenaic stadium has recently been incorporated into the official design of Olympic medals, thus foregrounding in visual terms the debt owed to the Greek capital by the Olympic movement as a whole.

Dancers performing for the Ballets Russes production of Milhaud's ballet *Le Train Bleu* in 1924.

three
A SUITABLE ACTIVITY FOR A WOMAN?

The ancient Olympic Games were always an exclusively male affair. Women were not only denied the right to participate in any of the athletic competitions but also, in all probability, even to attend as spectators.[1] As Pausanias recounted, the local Eleans had instituted a law proclaiming that any woman found in attendance at the Games would be thrown from the nearby cliffs.[2] Only the symbolic presence of the priestess of Demeter Chamyne ensured any female presence during Olympic festivals. There were, however, a few occasions on which women either overcame or circumvented these exclusions. Kyniska of Sparta, for example, was famously declared the first woman to win an Olympic victory following her success in the chariot race. It should be added, however, that the prize for this event was conferred upon the owner of the horses rather than the charioteer and thus, Kyniska's victory came despite the fact that she was not allowed to attend the Games. This did not prevent her father and brothers from erecting a victory statue dedicated to her in the sanctuary at Olympia. A second woman, Kallipateira (sometimes referred to as Pherenike) is said to have illicitly attended the Games disguised as a man in order to watch her son compete. Exhilarated by the victory of her offspring, she jumped a fence and was, quite literally, exposed as a woman. She escaped punishment, however, on the grounds that she came

from the family of Diagoras of Rhodes, a renowned athletic dynasty that had produced three generations of Olympic victors.[3]

All this did not, of course, mean that women were excluded from all forms of sport and exercise in the ancient world. It is known, for example, that young Spartan women frequently undertook physical training alongside men as a means to improve their strength and endurance. These exercises, according to Plutarch, specifically included activities associated with the Games, such as running, wrestling and throwing both the javelin and the discus.[4] Further, Pausanias records that athletic contests limited exclusively to women also took place at Olympia, though not at the same time as the larger, exclusively male event. This so-called Heraia, or festival of Hera, was similarly staged every four years and involved foot races with olive wreaths awarded to the victor. Unlike their male counterparts, the young women ran shorter distances and were partially clothed, wearing short dresses attached at the shoulder and leaving the right breast exposed.[5] Two archaeological finds have been associated with this early female sporting activity: a marble copy of a fifth-century-BC bronze representing a female runner, now in the Vatican Museum in Rome; and a small, bronze statuette of a female runner in the collection of the British Museum

Bronze figure of a running Spartan girl, 6th century BC.

in London. While there is still some dispute concerning the extent to which these works can be interpreted as representations of competitors at the Heraia, they nonetheless provide evidence for the kind of physical activities practiced by women at this early age.

Women Competitors at the Modern Olympics

When the fledgling IOC re-launched the Olympic Games in 1896, its members broadly concurred with the ancient attitude towards women participants, though not even Coubertin conceived of banning women spectators. Accordingly, not a single women's event was held during the first Games of the modern era despite, or perhaps as a consequence of, growing support for women's suffrage movements in both Britain and the United States. It is also highly likely that things would have stayed this way had the IOC been able to enforce its will. Coubertin, certainly, was openly against women participating in the Games, arguing that they were physically unsuited to excessively vigorous exercise and that 'their particular role should be that of crowning the champions'.[6] Coubertin's main concern seems to have been to maintain his notion of propriety. Thus he explicitly claimed in 1922 that, while the majority of spectators at male sporting events were there to 'watch the sport', those attending women's events might 'do so for reasons having little to do with sport'.[7] For Coubertin, it seems, the voyeuristic eye of the spectator was confined exclusively to the male gender and was focused solely on the female athlete.

Despite the views both of Coubertin and the IOC, women did compete at the Games of the second Olympiad in Paris in 1900 and have done so at every Games thereafter. This early inclusion of women, however, can hardly be read as a sign of emancipation or tolerance. Rather, it came about more as a consequence of the IOC handing over power to local organizers who adopted a fairly casual attitude to the question of women's participation.[8] Even then, the numbers were negligible, with only 22 women competing in Paris and just six at the St Louis Games of 1904. Moreover, this participation was restricted to sports regarded as more genteel, such as archery, croquet, golf and tennis.[9]

Imaging Female Victors

Certainly the most famous of the women victors at the Paris Games was the British tennis player, Charlotte (popularly known as 'Chattie') Cooper. By 1900, Cooper

Charlotte Cooper, the First Woman to Win an Olympic Gold Medal (at the 1900 Paris Olympic Games). Here Photographed after her Victory at Wimbledon in 1908.

The French Tennis Player Hélène Prévost, Silver Medallist at the 1900 Paris Olympic Games. Reproduced in *La Vie au Grand Air* magazine (1900).

was already a three-time Wimbledon champion, having secured the title in 1895, 1896 and 1898. In Paris she secured victory with relative ease, defeating her French opponent Hélène Prévost 6–4, 6–2 in the final. Later that same day she secured a second Olympic title by winning the mixed doubles competition with fellow British tennis player Reginald Doherty. Contemporary reports suggest that Cooper's game was wide-ranging and that she possessed a formidable backhand. Also in her armoury was the capacity to volley and smash the ball. She was thus ever-willing to approach the net, something her singles opponent constantly refrained from attempting.[10] In an era when the women's game

was more noted for its grace and elegance than energy and dynamism, Cooper appears to have been one of the instigators of the more physical approach to women's tennis, and sport in general, that would come to fruition in the inter-war years. Cooper's appearance was notably captured in a semi-action photograph reproduced in the French sports journal *La Vie au Grand Air*. Here she is seen poised on her toes, racquet in hand and glancing in the direction in which she has, in all likelihood, just hit the ball. Yet what is perhaps most striking about this photograph is the costume worn by Cooper. Ankle-length skirts, a corseted waistband and long sleeves were very much the order of the day for female tennis players, attire hardly conducive to energetic physical movement. Moreover, the puffed shoulders and belt and collar arrangement clearly indicate a prioritizing of fashion and style over sporting function. Notably, *La Vie au Grand Air* also carried an illustration of Cooper's defeated opponent, Prévost, represented in a simple standing pose that makes no concession to the athletic activity with which she is associated. The inclusion of a decorative bow at the neck and a *canotier* (or straw boater) serves further to undermine the sense of physicality and strength necessary for athletic endeavour.

Throughout her career, the popular image of Cooper would also be straightjacketed into this conventional, passive mode of representation. Hence the most widely deployed image of the first-ever female Olympic victor is a photograph taken around 1908 when Cooper won her fifth Wimbledon title at 37 years of age. Despite her earlier Olympic victory and her formidable record at the Wimbledon championships, the photographer here made little concession to the fact that Cooper was at the apex of her athletic achievements. Her white costume and racquet, as attribute, certainly confirms her status as a tennis player, though perhaps only to signify the game as a suitable social activity for a middle-class woman. Cooper, now widely known as Mrs Alfred Sterry, was thus posed before a conventional studio landscape backdrop. Her high collar, adorned with a striped club tie, and the ivy-clad wooden fence upon which she leans, all seem designed to confine rather than liberate Cooper's movement, while the emphasis placed on her wedding ring serves to affirm her status as married woman as much as tennis player. This rather stiff mode of representation conformed, of course, to wider Edwardian conventions for the representation of women, as well as pandering to

the demand for both physical and sartorial propriety that appealed to Coubertin and the IOC. Within a decade and a half, however, women's tennis, not least at the Olympic Games of Antwerp 1920 and Paris 1924, would dramatically cast off this image of restraint and confinement, while simultaneously blazing a trail for women athletes in other Olympic sports.

Anyone for Tennis?

The new image of the sportswoman that emerged in the 1920s owed much to the wider sociological and cultural shifts of the early inter-war era. Throughout Western Europe and the United States, many women were reluctant to relinquish the, albeit limited, independence they had gained as a consequence of entering the workforce during the First World War, while suffrage movements were also making inroads into establishing more equitable voting rights for women. New attitudes challenged the conventionally accepted roles for women and the concept of the 'new woman' became part of a wider public discourse. In popular culture, the so-called 'flapper' came to be identified as one manifestation of this shift in expectation, behaviour and appearance among a younger generation of women on both sides of the Atlantic. Renowned as an iconoclast and a libertarian, the 'flapper' flouted convention by indulging openly in activities previously considered the exclusive domain of men. In physical appearance she was recognized as sporting bobbed hair, straight dresses cut high at the leg and exotic headgear. On stage and screen she was personified by celebrities such as Josephine Baker, Louise Brooks and Clara Bow. Sport, however, also played a vital role in the popular identity of the thoroughly modern woman of the 1920s and few sporting activities encapsulated

Suzanne Lenglen, Gold Medallist at the 1920 Antwerp Olympic Games.

the fashion-consciousness and style of the Jazz Age more than tennis.

In 1920, a young Frenchwoman named Suzanne Lenglen entered the women's tennis competition at the Antwerp Olympic Games. The previous year, she had achieved a hard-fought victory in her first international tournament, defeating the more favoured Dorothea Lambert Chambers 10–8, 4–6, 9–7 in the longest Wimbledon final to date. As Jennifer Hargreaves has pointed out, Lenglen's victory offered a stark vision of the contrast between the old and the new in women's sport in the post-war era.[11] At 40, Lambert Chambers was twice the age of her young opponent. More importantly, she personified the Edwardian

notion of sporting femininity. A contemporary of Charlotte Cooper, Lambert Chambers appeared on court in long dresses, closely tied at the waist and with long sleeves that ensured her arms remained fully covered at all times. Lenglen, in contrast, shocked the crowds at Wimbledon by wearing sleeveless silk dresses cut to above calf-length, over white stockings rolled at the knee. Lenglen, it should be added, was not the first female tennis player to expose an ankle or an arm. In 1912 her compatriot Marguerite Broquedis won the women's tennis competition at the Stockholm Olympic Games dressed in a stylish, short-sleeved top and a skirt cut a little higher than convention allowed. To celebrate her victory, the journal *Fémina* published a photograph of Broquedis in full stride on the cover of its edition of 15 August. Here, Broquedis' more modern appearance certainly challenged conventional female tennis attire and comportment, although her tight waistband and fashionable cloche hat still signify a greater emphasis on fashion than sporting functionality. Broquedis' flouting of convention, however, paled into insignificance compared with Lenglen's. The latter's more loosely fitting sportswear allowed her to leap around the court from baseline to net, stretching for shots that would previously have been left as unreachable, and thus to exploit her extraordinary physical agility. This, as was frequently noted, resulted in a frank exposure of parts of the female body that had hitherto not been seen in women's tennis.

'Marguerite Broquedis, Olympic Tennis Champion, 1912', from the cover of *Femina* magazine (15 August 1912).

'La Divine' Suzanne

At the Antwerp Games of 1920, Lenglen followed up her Wimbledon success by winning two gold medals (singles and mixed doubles) and a bronze (women's doubles), thus establishing her reputation as a world-beater. Olympic victory also enhanced her status as an icon for the ever-expanding mass media audience. Instantly recognizable by her trademark bandeau headwear, risqué dresses and balletic movements, Lenglen was dubbed 'La Divine' and rapidly acquired notoriety as a flamboyant celebrity. Her feisty character, alongside the fact that she frequently sipped cognac between sets, only served to reinforce her public image as the very epitome of the 'flapper'. By now, functionality was not the only hallmark of Lenglen's dresses. Specially designed by the couturier Jean Patou, Lenglen's sportswear signified the very height of Parisian fashion and heralded a new taste for women's clothes. Indeed, the extent to which sporting costumes for both men and women acquired an *haute couture* status may be measured by the fact that in 1925 Patou opened a fashion boutique called 'Le Coin des Sports' in which each room was dedicated to an individual sport. Two years later, the Italian fashion designer Elsa Schiaparelli followed suit by opening a Paris boutique, 'Pour le sport', while the image of the modern sportswoman dominated fashion magazines.[12] The fashionable image of sporting femininity was also exploited by the artist Tamara de Lempicka, whose paintings of young women in sports settings were widely exhibited throughout the 1920s.

To enhance her status as a representative of ultra-modernity, Lenglen was frequently photographed in Patou costumes, whether sporting or otherwise. More significantly, her image was also exploited in other visual media as a signifier of the post-war modern woman. In 1921, for example, an illustration

Suzanne Lenglen wearing a dress by Jean Patou (1926).

implies that this is a nocturnal game while the flushed cheeks of both Lenglen and her partner suggest an overall sense of exhilaration. Vincent's illustration seems less concerned to portray Lenglen as a competitive and highly successful sportswoman than to celebrate the notion of gilded youth at play.

In a similar vein, Armand Vallée's illustration for *La Vie Parisienne* also focuses on Lenglen both as pleasure-seeker and object of the male gaze far more than serious sporting competitor. *La première raquette de France – Suzanne aux bains . . . de mer* (The number one tennis player in France – Suzanne bathing . . . in the sea) once again removes Lenglen from the specialist arena of the tennis court, placing her instead in the fashionable surroundings of a Mediterranean seaside resort. Her sporting efforts, again

on the cover of *La Vie au grand air* by Réné Vincent represented Lenglen dressed in a white, flowing dress and yellow jacket with matching bandeau. Here, Lenglen's abilities as a tennis player notably play second fiddle to her purported status as party-girl. Though best known for her singles play, Lenglen is shown in partnership with a young male player while simultaneously being watched by a handsome, young umpire. Posed casually, with his foot on the net, this official's eyes seem more trained on Lenglen's figure than the passage of the ball. The midnight blue background, with tennis ball doubling up as a lunar heavenly body illuminating the sky, additionally

René Vincent, 'Tennis with Mademoiselle Suzanne Lenglen', illustration from *La Vie au Grand Air* (1921).

in a mixed doubles context, are here reduced to little more than an upper-class leisure pursuit akin to that of the bathers inhabiting the background. The title, referring to Suzanne bathing, is intended as a pun, alluding to the biblical tale of Susanna and the Elders, in which a beautiful young woman is gazed upon voyeuristically by lecherous older men. Thus Lenglen's lithe and athletic body, attenuated in Vallée's illustration to match the popular conventions for the representation of the modern woman in contemporary fashion illustrations, is reduced to little more than eye candy to be consumed by an insatiable audience. In some contexts, at least, Coubertin's anxieties regarding the potential lascivious gaze of so-called sports spectators, seem to have had some foundation.

Following her success at the Antwerp Games, Lenglen rapidly established her status as the world's number one female tennis player. Four years later she looked set to repeat her Olympic triumph, this time on her native soil, during the Paris Games of 1924. Shortly before the competition began, however, she was forced to withdraw, having been diagnosed with jaundice and an enlarged liver.[13] The absence of the most famous sporting celebrity in France was clearly a blow to the organizers of the Games. Nonetheless, Lenglen could be said to have made one important, if oblique, appearance during the Paris Olympic Games. On 24 June 1924, in the midst of the Games and less than three weeks before the tennis competition was due to commence, the Théâtre des Champs-Elysées premiered a new production by Sergei Diaghilev's *Ballets Russes*. *Le Train bleu* was a short ballet based on an idea by Jean Cocteau, choreographed by Bronislava Nijinska and with music by Darius Milhaud, sets by Henri Laurens, costumes by Gabrielle ('Coco') Chanel and a stage curtain by Pablo Picasso. Set on the Mediterranean coast it featured the fashionable set

at play as characterized by a corps de ballet of bathers, supporting the principal dancers, including a male golfer and a female tennis player. The former of these was widely understood to represent the then Prince of Wales, later Duke of Windsor.[14] The latter was clearly a paean to Lenglen, whose infamous sporting movements were exquisitely choreographed into balletic arabesques, jetés and pirouettes, all performed against a backdrop of sun and sea. In this context, Lenglen's achievements were openly and sympathetically celebrated, not just as indicative of sporting victory, but also as an expression of sheer artistry.

Poker Face

While Lenglen's absence from the tennis competition at the Paris Olympic Games was widely regretted, it did at least open the door for the emergence of a new tennis sensation. Helen Wills was yet to complete her studies at the University of California, Berkeley, when she arrived in Paris. Nonetheless, the American teenager cruised to Olympic victory without dropping a set. Like Lenglen before her, she doubled her tally of Olympic gold medals, winning the women's doubles. Also like Lenglen, Wills was instantly recognizable on court, although both her costume and comportment differed radically from the elder Frenchwoman's. Lenglen's chic Patou dresses and exotic bandeau here gave way to the more staid sailor-suit outfits and functional sun-visor of the younger player. And while Lenglen was celebrated both for her artistic temperament and her grace and elegance, Wills was admired more for a focus and steely determination that resulted in her being dubbed 'poker face' in the popular press.[15]

Wills's victory in Paris made her a serious contender for Lenglen's crown. However, the two

Alexander Calder, *Helen Wills*, 1927, wire and wood.

Olympic champions were to compete in a singles match together just once, two years later, in a specially arranged tournament at the Carlton Club in Cannes. The 'match of the century', as the contest was popularly dubbed, attracted worldwide press attention and intense negotiations between newsreel companies for the broadcasting rights.[16] Lenglen's 6–3, 8–6 straight sets victory affirmed her superiority but was seen to be a struggle for the older player. Shortly after this victory, Lenglen turned professional and the two greatest women tennis players of the era never competed against each other again. Following this monumental battle, the world's media attention was increasingly focused upon Wills, who now took over the mantle of the most famous sportswoman of her era. In this guise she was regularly featured in the popular press and twice illustrated on the cover of *Time* magazine during the 1920s.[17] Wills also attracted the attention of major artists. In 1927, for example,

Alexander Calder produced one of his trademark wire sculptures representing Wills in full flight. Calder was working in Paris at this time and was clearly swept up by the publicity surrounding the Lenglen versus Wills showdown. His representation, though identifiable as Wills by the inclusion of the signature sun-visor, might perhaps be read more as an amalgamation of both players, not least because the graceful, balletic pose clearly recalls the familiar image of Lenglen as captured in action photographs of the period.

In August 1932 Wills was also illustrated by the Mexican artist and illustrator Miguel Covarrubias for the cover of *Vanity Fair.* Here the sinuous curves and floating grace of the balletic Lenglen are replaced by a more angular and jagged mode of depiction. Again depicted wearing her trademark visor and further identified by the initials 'HW' emblazoned across her chest, Wills is represented more as a physically strong and determined player, commanding both the net

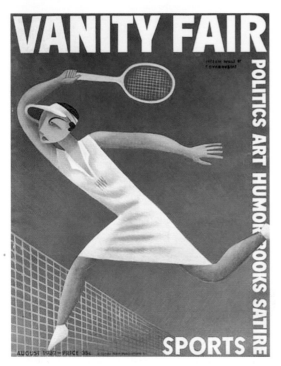

Miguel Covarrubias, 'Helen Wills', illustration on cover of *Vanity Fair* (August 1932).

presence would also characterize the most famous representation of Wills, executed as part of Diego Rivera's mural, *Allegory of California*, installed on the staircase of the San Francisco Stock Exchange in 1931. The towering figure of Wills dominates Rivera's composition, though represented not as herself, but as an earth goddess, a personification of the agricultural and mineral riches of the Californian lands. The decision to cast Wills in this light caused much controversy at the time of the unveiling of Rivera's mural, reflecting the extent to which the image of Wills was reaching beyond that of simply tennis player, sportswoman

Diego Rivera, *Allegory of California (detail with monumental portrait of Helen Wills)*, 1931, fresco, Pacific Stock Exchange, San Francisco.

and the attention of the spectator. The full swing of her racquet-arm implies a powerful shot while the concentrated and strained expression on her Cubist-style, half-profile face further suggests a ruthless competitor at the top of her game. Covarrubias was not alone in shifting the emphasis from grace and elegance to power and presence in his representations of Wills. In 1927 the Armenian-born, California-based artist Haig Patigian was commissioned to produce a marble portrait bust of Wills. Stripped of the usual attributes signifying Wills as tennis player, Patigian's bust instead emphasized personality. Here Wills is represented as an intensely focused and determined individual, whose erectly held head, firm jaw and purposeful gaze exudes self-assurance. This same and Olympic champion. Here the individual purposefulness and self-possession that were integral to her sporting success are celebrated as qualities intrinsically valuable in their own right.

Lenglen and Wills, both Olympic champions in their day, transformed women's tennis, not only through their relative styles of play, but also as a consequence of the popular public image that emerged of each sportswoman. Yet both remained essentially participants in a sport that had long accepted women participants. To challenge the more widely held notion that other sports were unsuitable activities for women, more radical interventions were required.

The Rise of the Women's Olympics

The number of women competing at each Olympic Games had slowly increased throughout the first quarter of the twentieth century. Nonetheless, this figure represented no more than 2.5 per cent of all competitors up to 1920, and peaked at only 4.5 per cent by the time of the Paris Games of 1924.[18] The introduction of figure skating at the London Games of 1908 and swimming and diving at Stockholm in 1912 expanded the number of events in which female athletes could compete, but women's sport remained largely marginal to the Olympic movement. This situation began to undergo something of a transformation when women's athletics were introduced into the Olympic programme for the first time at the Amsterdam Games of 1928. Once again, this more tolerant attitude towards the inclusion of women's sport emerged less as a consequence of the IOC's desire to change its original stance than through the emergence of outside forces, in this case an independent and highly successful international sporting movement headed by the Frenchwoman Alice Milliat.

A translator by trade and rower by passion, Milliat's love of sport may well have emerged during the years she spent in England as a young woman. Once back in her native France, she joined Fémina Sport, an organization first established in 1912 to promote the participation of women in a wide range of sports including cycling, football and rugby.[19] Fémina Sport continued its activities throughout the First World War and even organized national athletic championships for women in 1917.[20] Inspired by the belief that women should not be debarred from participation in any form of labour or leisure activity, Milliat soon rose to a position of prominence within the women's sport movement and, by March 1919, had been unanimously elected President of the Fédération des Sociétés Féminines Sportives de France (FSFSF).[21] Shortly after taking up this post, Milliat approached the IOC and proposed an expansion of women's competitions for the Antwerp Games of 1920. When this was resisted she set about organizing an alternative event, an international athletics tournament for women, to be held in Monte Carlo in 1921. This proved a great success, not least by attracting considerable media attention. Milliat's next step was to establish a new administrative body, the Fédération Sportive Féminine Internationale (FSFI), which immediately set about organizing what came to be known as the First Women's Olympic Games, held in 1922.

'La première olympiade féminine', took place on 20 August at the Pershing Stadium in Paris and attracted athletes from Czechoslovakia, France, Britain, Switzerland and the United States. A reported crowd of 15,000 were in attendance for the one-day event, which commenced with an official opening ceremony at which the competitors marched behind their national flags.[22] The Games drew widespread media coverage, both during the build-up and following the event, with

Mildred 'Babe' Didrikson, Shortly After Setting a World Record in the Javelin Competition at the 1932 Los Angeles Olympic Games.

Without doubt, the most famous female track and field athlete in Olympic history remains the Dutchwoman Fanny Blankers-Koen. In 1948 Blankers-Koen won four gold medals at the first post-war Games in London (80-metre hurdles, 100 metres, 200 metres and 4 x 100 metres), a record that stands to this day. As Olympic regulations prevented athletes from competing in more than four events, she did not compete in the long jump or high jump, despite being the world record holder in both events at the

time. Having made her first unsuccessful Olympic appearance at the Berlin Games in 1936, Blankers-Koen's chances of Olympic glory seemed to have fallen victim to political circumstance, with both the proposed 1940 and 1944 Games, planned for Tokyo and London respectively, being cancelled during the Second World War. In more favourable circumstances, the Games of 1948 might well have been Blankers-Koen's fourth. Now 30 years of age, she remained a top-flight athlete, but was dismissed by many as

Han Rehm, *Monument to Fanny Blankers-Koen*, 1954, bronze; in Rotterdam.

being too old. What was most striking for contemporary commentators, and clearly disturbing for some, was not her age, but the fact that she was by now a mother of two and, although not widely known during the games, pregnant with her third child at the time she competed.[32] Problematically, Blankers-Koen was widely presented in the popular press through her 'matronly' attributes. For example, the *Daily Graphic* highlighted the Dutch athlete's 'artistry' in darning socks and declared that her 'greatest love, next to

racing, is housework'.[33] In a similar vein she was popularly dubbed the 'Flying Housewife'. Yet, despite these media attempts to contain Blankers-Koen within conventional notions of femininity, her success was instrumental in disproving the then popularly held view that maternity and elite athletic performance were incompatible. Blankers-Koen's achievements made her both a national and an international icon. In her native Netherlands she had a major stadium and annual Games named in her honour and in 1999 her historical reputation was further enhanced when she was declared female athlete of the century by the International Association of Athletics Federations (IAAF). Nonetheless, Blankers-Koen's status as an Olympic sporting icon has remained inextricably linked to her biological condition as mother.

There have, however, been exceptions to this conventional mode of representation. In the early 1950s, the Dutch artist Han Rehm was commissioned to produce a monument to Blankers-Koen to be erected in Rotterdam. Significantly, Rehm drew inspiration less from Blankers-Koen's maternal reputation than from a well-known photograph showing the victorious Dutch athlete crossing the finishing line during the 4 x 100-metre relay race at the London Olympic Games. Here, the emphasis is notably on physical effort, resilience and endurance, despite the fact that the victory has come in a short-distance, speed event. Blankers-Koen is thus represented in full stride, with limp arms and head thrown back in a gesture of exhaustion. This representation certainly articulates the endurance demanded of an older athlete. At the same time, however, the fatigue explicitly fore-grounded in this monument seems also to echo the wider historical circumstances in which Blankers-Koen's victory was achieved. Dubbed the Austerity Games, the Olympics of 1948 were held amidst the early stages of the reconstruction of Europe after the devastation of the Second World War. With food rationing still in place and the memory of the privations endured by millions during the conflict still in the forefront of the popular imagination, stoicism, fortitude and endurance were familiar and admired qualities. Hence, it is perhaps unsurprising that the other visual icon of the 1948 Games was the Czech runner, Emil Zátopek, an athlete whose capacity to endure the pain and suffering of long distance

running was etched into every muscle of his seemingly frail physique and physiognomy. Blankers-Koen, too, was celebrated for her capacity to endure, a factor made all the more significant by the near starvation conditions that she and many of her compatriots had been forced to endure during the so-called hunger-winter of 1944. Commissioned in the immediate post-war era for a city virtually destroyed by the Luftwaffe, Rehm's monument to international sporting victory can thus be read more widely as symbolic of the endurance and survival of the Dutch nation, here personified in the figure of Blankers-Koen. Erected around the same time as Osip Zadkine's more famous Rotterdam monument, 'The Destroyed City', Rehm's sculpture reveals how representations of individual Olympic sportsmen and women can operate as far more than simple celebrations of individual achievement.

The Struggle Continues

During the latter part of the twentieth century, the participation of women at the Olympics continued to grow as the Games increasingly became a global sporting phenomenon. As the Cold War intensified, the successes of Soviet and Eastern European female athletes contributed to more concerted efforts to support and strengthen women's sport though, as shall be seen in chapter Five, this was more evident in the East than the West. Furthermore, the rise of the feminist movement in the 1970s and the introduc-tion of legislation demanding equality of opportunity contributed to something of a transformation in the landscape of women's sport. By the Sydney Games of 2000, for example, women's participation in the Olympic Games had risen to just over 38 per cent, having barely broken the 10 per cent mark in the pre-Second World War era. This figure increased

Fanny Blankers-Koen Winning the Last Lap of the 400 metres Relay Final at the 1948 London Olympic Games.

British heptathlete Jessica Ennis competing at the 20th European Athletics Championships in Barcelona, 30 July 2010.

to more than 40 per cent at the Athens Games of 2004 and 42 per cent at the Beijing Games of 2008. In addition, by this latter stage, only two sports specifically excluded women from participating: baseball and boxing. As baseball has now been dropped for the 2012 Games in London, and women's boxing will be featured for the first time, the London Games will be the first with no sports excluding women. Yet the dominant male hegemony of international sporting federations, including the IOC, still remains a bone of contention. Before 1981, for example, IOC membership was exclusively male and even as late as 2005 less than 10 per cent of the IOC membership was female. And while recent efforts have been made to address this, the percentage of women IOC members at the start of 2011 was still only around 17 per cent.[34]

Although women's sport is now successfully competing for attention alongside men's at the Olympics, the image of the female athlete has hardly changed. For example, since the conclusion of the Beijing Games, media debates have focused on the question of who might be the 'face of London 2012' with athletes Jessica Ennis and Christine Ohuruogu making the early front-running. However, the widespread media use of terminology such as 'poster-girl' and 'pin-up' certainly suggest that physical attractiveness may be more valued in these arenas than athletic ability.[35] Women's sport at the Olympic Games has come a long way since the total exclusion at the Athens Games in 1896 and the reluctant tolerance of the inter-war years. The extent to which the popular image of the female athlete in visual culture has altered, in line with changes in social attitudes, remains an issue of some debate.

Armand Vallée, 'La Première Racquette de France, Suzanne aux Bains . . . de Mer', illustration from *La Vie Parisienne* magazine (1921).

The gymnastics competition. Still from the official film shot during the 1908 London Olympic Games.

The tug-of-war contest. Still from the official film shot during the 1908 London Olympic Games.

four
CELLULOID GAMES

When the inaugural Olympic Games of the modern era were staged in Athens in April 1896, barely three months had passed since the Lumière brothers had famously held their first public screening of the new cinematographic medium at the Grand Café on Boulevard des Capucines in Paris. Thus the birth and rise of the modern Games is virtually coterminous with that of cinema. Given this coincidental alignment it is perhaps surprising that no known footage exists of the first two Olympic competitions in Athens and Paris, and only fragments from the third Games in St Louis.[1] In 1906, at the Intercalary Games in Athens, at least one movie camera was in operation, as evidenced by a 30-second extract showing the standing high jump.[2] Two years later, however, this paucity of cinematic interest was somewhat rectified when the French production company, Pathé Frères shot extensive scenes from the Games for its newly instigated newsreel programmes. Thus the Games of the fourth Olympiad in London were the first to be widely recorded in moving pictures. From this point on movie, and later television, cameras became an ever-present feature of Olympic festivals, capturing the drama and excitement of the spectacle and disseminating this to wide audiences across the globe.

Much of this footage provides fascinating visual evidence regarding the early Olympic Games. For example, past events long discontinued, such as the tug-of-war and the standing long jump and high jump, were documented at the London Games of 1908.[3] Similarly, shifting attitudes towards appropriate sportswear are made evident, a startling example being the abundance not only of bandanas, but also flat caps and even pith helmets, worn by marathon runners at the Stockholm Games in 1912.[4] These early films, however, rarely set out to achieve much more than document the events for posterity. Given the limitations of the technology at the time, cameras were typically set up to shoot from a single viewpoint, often in close proximity to a given activity. Conventions for filming the Olympics soon emerged and shots of competitors marching at the opening ceremony, joyful crowds cheering, dignitaries arriving at the stadium, runners crossing the finishing line and athletes performing the long or high jump, or throwing the javelin, discus or shot-put, rapidly became the stock-in-trade of early sports cinematography.

In 1924 filming the Games reached a new level when the French cinematographer Jean de Rovera produced two feature films for public release. The first of these recorded events was the Games held at Chamonix, later designated the first winter Olympics; the second, competitions in Paris, including the famous victories of Harold Abrahams and Eric Liddell, later immortalized

OH, DEM GOLDEN STOCKINGS! THE CREAM-AND-GOLD CONTINGENT OF SUPERB DANISH GIRLS JUMPING AT THE OLYMPIC GAMES.

Danish athletes at the 1908 London Olympic games; from *The Sketch* (July 1908).

in the cinematic dramatization of 1981, *Chariots of Fire*. By now, it was increasingly recognized that recording the Games on celluloid was a lucrative business and newsreel companies fought each other to obtain filming rights from the various organizing committees.[5] When in 1932 the Games were held in Los Angeles, the proximity of the Hollywood studios seemed to provide an ideal opportunity for a new, more cinematographically inspired, approach to filming the Games. Certainly there was talk of making a major film based on the copious footage shot by the

various newsreel companies licensed to record the event, but this, in the end came to nothing.[6] Thus it would not be in the movie capital of the world, but in National Socialist Berlin, four years later, that the first innovative documentary recording the Olympic Games would be produced.

The Triumph of 'Olympia'

Germany had been excluded from participating in the Olympic Games at both Antwerp (1920) and Paris (1924) as punishment for its role in the First World War. While some nations remained unhappy about ever letting the former enemy back into the Olympic fold, international attitudes had begun to change by the late 1920s, and a German team was thus invited to take part in the Games in Amsterdam in 1928. Three years later, this gesture of goodwill was extended when the IOC announced that the Games of the eleventh Olympiad in 1936 would be held in Berlin. As the lost Games of 1916 had originally been scheduled to take place in the German capital, this seemed an appropriate recompense for the then Weimar Republic. Yet within two years of this announcement political circumstances had altered radically. When the National Socialist Party assumed power in the spring of 1933, the future of the Berlin Games initially appeared far from certain. The cosmopolitan and pacifist agenda of the IOC hardly sat comfortably with the new regime while the significant presence of left-wing workers' sports movements in Germany and Austria (Frankfurt and Vienna had hosted the first two workers' Olympiads in 1925 and 1931) made the National Socialists far from at ease with international sports festivals. Nonetheless, the authorities quickly recognized the potential of the Games to showcase the new Germany. Accordingly, the state

machinery of the Third Reich swiftly took control of all matters related to the staging of the Games while the new Chancellor, Adolf Hitler, even made a personal intervention, proposing that plans for the stadium and sports complex be expanded considerably.[7] From the moment the National Socialists took charge, the Berlin Games of 1936 were planned to be the biggest and most spectacular Games of the modern era.

Even as the summer of 1936 approached, however, a shadow of uncertainty remained cast over the proposed spectacle. Several sports organizations, especially in Britain and the United States, vehemently protested that the National Socialist regime was attempting to exploit the Games for political ends and thus threatened a boycott. The biggest objection, unsurprisingly, was against the new regime's racial policy, not least the exclusion of Jewish, and other non-Aryan, sportsmen and women from membership in official clubs. Opposition to the Games was much in evidence in the popular press. In July 1935, for example, *The Times* published a cartoon under the heading 'Olympic Games in Berlin!' in which goose-stepping Nazi sportsmen are shown marching over the body of 'The Olympic Spirit'. The axe of 'Nazi Justice' has here been plunged into the bleeding trunk of 'Sport' while Catholics, Jews and trade unionists are forced to watch from behind the bars of a concentration camp. While the swastika armbands and Heil Hitler salutes of the marching sportsmen certainly identify them as Nazis, it is noteworthy that the artist has here placed emphasis on football, cricket and tennis, three of Britain's most popular sporting pursuits. As tennis was no longer an Olympic sport and cricket had only been included once

Title page of an illegal KPD brochure, Paris, 1936.

'Olympic Games in Berlin', cartoon published in *The Times* (25 July 1935).

– mostly for British ex-patriots at the Paris Games of 1900 – the critique is clearly aimed at British Nazi sympathizers. In a similarly critical mode, the title page of an undercover German Communist Party booklet, bearing the slogan 'Olympiade in Berlin?' represented a muscular javelin thrower wearing an athletic vest with a swastika obscuring the five-ring symbol of the Olympic movement. This image is notably a modification of an earlier design for the Paris Games of 1924. However, as the athlete in the Berlin image prepares to throw his javelin, he casts the shadow of a grenade-wielding storm-trooper, thus amplifying the militaristic underpinnings of sport under National Socialism and equating the staging of the Games with the expansionist policies of Germany. Despite these protests, the political pressure put to bear on the German authorities had little impact, though it did result in the inclusion of two Jewish participants in the German Olympic team: Rudi Ball, an ice hockey player, and Helene Mayer, the Olympic fencing champion from the Games of 1928. This, however, was widely perceived as little more than window dressing to appease the threat of boycotts. In the end, all the major sporting nations agreed to compete at the Berlin Games. Republican Spain alone maintained a boycott, and even organized an alternative Workers' Games to be staged one week before the launch of the Berlin Olympics. The outbreak of the Spanish Civil War on the eve of the proposed contest rapidly put paid to these plans.[8]

In February 1936 the winter Games, held in the Bavarian mountains at Garmisch-Partenkirchen,

provided something of a dress rehearsal for the grander summer spectacle. Following this, carefully stage-managed events such as the lighting of the Olympic flame in the sanctuary of Olympia and the inaugural torch run carrying the sacred flame to Berlin, conferred a sense of pomp and ceremony on the preparations for the Games themselves and grabbed the attention of the world's media. Yet it is as a consequence of one particular intervention in the field of visual culture that the Berlin Games of 1936 are best remembered, and remain to this day such a hotly debated topic for political, sport and cultural historians. For, as the Games took place, dozens of cameramen descended on the various sports venues where they were being held. Hunkered

Berlin Panoramic parade at the 1936 Berlin Olympic Games.

Leni Riefenstahl and camera crew during the filming of *Olympia* in 1936.

down in specially dug out pits, stood aloft on purpose built towers and even floating overhead in specially commissioned balloons, this army shot over 250 hours of footage, all destined to be at the disposal of Leni Riefenstahl, the producer of the most famous sport documentary of all time. Riefenstahl's *Olympia* was the best part of a year in preparation, was subsequently shot in two weeks (the duration of the Games), and took a further year and a half to edit into what became a three-hour-long production. Divided into two parts (*Festival of Nations* and *Festival of Beauty*), Riefenstahl's *Olympia* proved to be a cinematographic record of the Olympic Games like no other.

Before working on *Olympia*, Riefenstahl had established a reputation as a much admired dancer and actress, starring in films such as *The Holy Mountain* (1926), *The White Hell of Piz Palu* (1929) and *Storm Over Mont Blanc* (1930). She was, however, far from content to remain an actress and sought to expand her cinematic knowledge and experience working alongside Arnold Fanck, the director of these so-called mountain films. In 1928, Fanck had been responsible for producing an Olympic documentary, *The White Stadium*, which recorded events at the second winter Games in St Moritz, and thus Riefenstahl drew on Fanck's knowledge and experience when planning how to shoot the Berlin Games. Though ostensibly produced as a documentary, *Olympia* went way beyond the simple reportage that had characterized earlier Olympic film footage. Indeed, Riefenstahl's aspirations were to produce a film that not only developed new means for recording sports action on film, but also of articulating new notions of how Olympic sport might both be conceived and experienced visually. At the time of its release in 1938 and subsequently, *Olympia* has been widely described in glowing artistic terms, as nothing less than 'a poem, a hymn, an ode to beauty', even a veritable sport-symphony.[9]

The most significant innovation in Reifenstahl's *Olympia* was the inclusion of a narrative prologue to both parts of the production. In *Festival of Nations*, for example, the first fifteen minutes are taken up with a scene-setting montage of images, shot by cameraman Willy Zielke, that take the viewer from the sites of ancient Greece to the heart of modern Berlin. As the opening titles fade, the camera pans across a desolate and misty landscape strewn with broken columns, lingering over these fragmented architectural remnants now overgrown with weeds. The absence of any signs of humanity adds to a broad sense that a long-forgotten land is about to be brought back to life. The plaintive strings of Herbert Windt's Wagnerian soundtrack add a further sense of mystery and melancholy to the scene as the music accompanies the camera, and thus the spectator, moving slowly and deliberately through doorways and around corners to discover ever-new vistas of a neglected antiquity. The emphasis on architectural detail soon gives way to a focus on statuary. Famous monuments (including the *Barberini Faun* and the *Medici Venus*) are dramatically lit and evocatively captured by a moving camera that effectively choreographs a Pygmalion-like resurrection of the ancient

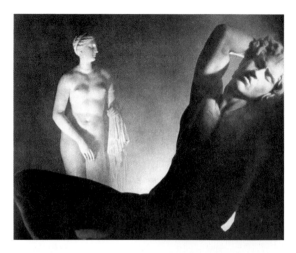

Still from Riefenstahl's *Olympia*, 1938: *Faun* and *Venus*.

marbles. Here, the spectator is presented with the concept of re-awakening, a re-birth from a long dormancy, an idea explicitly articulated in what is perhaps the most famous sequence from Riefenstahl's *Olympia*. As the camera rotates around a plaster replica of Myron's *Discobolus* (acquired specially for the film production), the image of a near-nude male athlete, adopting the same posture, is superimposed on the classical model. Thus the statue literally comes to life and performs, in slow and exquisitely choreographed motion, the physical rotations of a discus thrower in action. This image gives way to a series of shots of similarly clad male athletes performing various sporting actions – hurling the discus, javelin and shot-put – all filmed from a low angle against a dark and dramatic sky. Next naked female forms appear, enacting gymnastic movements either individually or in groups, the whole set in a natural landscape of wind-swept grasses and still seas, before flames rise from the bottom of the screen to engulf the entire scene.

While these scenes are certainly intended to evoke the ancient Olympic Games, they notably make no claim to historical accuracy. The architectural shots,

Marshall Wayne winning a gold medal in high diving at the 1936 Olympic Games, Berlin.

the jerkiness of the movements and to emphasize a smoother, floating quality to this dramatic physical action. Other experimental techniques employed by Riefenstahl include the use of shadows in both the fencing competition and the marathon to stand in for the sporting performers themselves. This serves to make the action both anonymous and dematerialized, once again destabilizing the viewer's sense of physical space. Notably, in her pursuit of specific effects, Riefenstahl showed little concern for the

veracity of the footage shot. Indeed, athletes were regularly asked to re-enact their performances to enable the camera to capture angles and close-ups that would not have been possible in real time. Two key examples of this are the use of a camera positioned as an oarsman in the boat for the rowing competition, and the frontal close-ups of swimmers taken from a rubber dinghy towed along ahead of the competitors. In both these instances, live competition footage is interspersed with shots taken during training to offer a more vivid, if doubtless contrived, sense of the overall action.

Following the premiere of *Olympia* in the spring of 1938, many critics on both sides of the Atlantic were effusive in their praise for Riefenstahl's achievement, despite widespread political reservations regarding the regime the film so explicitly served. In France, for example, *Le Figaro* claimed that *Olympia* was 'a master-piece which deserves to be ranked amongst the most famous', while in Los Angeles it was described as 'a triumph of the camera and an epic of the screen', despite the fact that it was not even given a general release in the United States.[12] *Olympia* was also showered with international prizes, including a gold medal at the Exposition Internationale in Paris in 1937, notably before the editing was completed, and a *grand prix* at the Venice Biennale the following year. In the aftermath of the Second World War, *Olympia* continued to attract positive critical responses. In 1948 it was awarded a diploma by the IOC and, a decade later, was declared one of the ten best films ever made.[13] Yet despite such fulsome praise, the film continues to be seen as profoundly flawed by its direct association with the National Socialist regime. Although Riefenstahl rigidly maintained claims to the contrary, it is clear that *Olympia* was not only financed by the Nazi party but also widely deployed by the regime for propaganda purposes. Further, while it could be argued that Riefenstahl's celebration of Olympic sport is far less explicit in its promotion of National Socialism than her equally famous cinematic celebration of the Nuremburg Rally in 1934, *Triumph of the Will*, it remains nonetheless virtually impossible to untangle *Olympia* from the political and ideological context in which it was produced. While there are certainly grounds for claims made by Riefenstahl apologists that Hitler is far from excessively celebrated in *Olympia*, and that if any one figure is given heroic

Leni Riefenstahl with a cameraman filming swimming action outside the Olympic competition in 1936, for *Olympia*.

75

status it is not an Aryan *übermensch*, but the African-American athlete Jesse Owens, this hardly results in a film that ends up, as Riefenstahl herself claimed, as purely artistic and apolitical.[14] Perhaps in the end, *Olympia* is best regarded as a conflicted and contradictory product of visual culture, an innovative, creative and compelling piece of cinematic theatre that transformed notions of how sport might be recorded on film, though simultaneously tainted by its implicit desire to celebrate some of the more problematic values associated with the National Socialist regime by whom, and for whom, it was essentially produced.

The Berlin Games of 1936 undoubtedly altered the landscape of the Olympic Games. After this, claims regarding the 'purity' of Olympism, or that the Games could operate independently of political and ideological agendas largely rang hollow; though it might be added that this did not prevent such claims being made on a regular basis. But it was not just the appropriation of the Games by the National Socialist regime that destabilized the foundation of the temple of Olympic idealism. It was also the increasing knowledge of the power of visual culture as a tool not so much for recording the Games as for shaping understandings of the values associated with them. Here, for example, it could be argued that the Berlin Games would not still be regarded as such an integral component within the National Socialist propaganda machine, were it not for Riefenstahl's particular intervention. *Olympia* shaped the public conception of the Games and, perhaps more importantly, continues to do so. At the same time it affirmed the importance of the official Olympic film as an integral element within the entire organizational process. Indeed, one of the legacies of Riefenstahl's project is the fact that since 1936, every Olympic Games has been recorded for posterity in

an officially commissioned and produced film. The vast majority of these, however, like the newsreels before them, unproblematically adopted established conventions of cinematic reportage.[15] One other Olympic film, however, deserves special mention both as a creative intervention into this process and as a direct response to the precedent set by Riefenstahl.

The Humanity of Defeat

The proposed Games of 1940 had originally been scheduled to be held in Tokyo but, as with Berlin a generation earlier, were cancelled due to the outbreak of war. After this it would be the best part of a quarter century before the Games would finally reach Japanese shores. In 1964, however, as the new Japan emerged from the rubble of defeat, the world's athletes and media descended upon Tokyo to celebrate the first Games to be held in Asia. Like all National Olympic Committees, the organizers of the Tokyo Games wished to present a glowing image of the nation and its capital to the world. To this end, they called upon their most famous cinematographer, Akira Kurosawa to produce the official film of the Games. After much preparatory work, however, Kurosawa fell into dispute with the organizing committee and withdrew, to be replaced at short notice by another stalwart of the Japanese cinematic renaissance of the post-war era, Kon Ichikawa. Like Riefenstahl before him, Ichikawa had access to vast resources, including an army of cameramen, and the most up-to-date technology, including Technicolor.[16] Despite this, the resultant film, *Tokyo Olympiad*, proved to be a disappointment to its commissioners. Rather than celebrate the nation's achievements and sporting victories (Japan finished third in the overall Olympic medals table, only being surpassed by the two super-powers, the

'The Re-enacted Torch Run in Front of Mount Fuji'; still from Kon Ichikawa, *Tokyo Olympiad* (1965).

United States and the Soviet Union) Ichikawa focused much more on the human drama of the Games.

Before shooting *Tokyo Olympiad*, Ichikawa studied Riefenstahl's iconic precedent in close detail, later referring to it as 'a textbook' from which he built the foundations for his own film.[17] As a consequence of this there are a number of key structural similarities between the two films. For example, Ichikawa notably constructed *Tokyo Olympiad* in two parts, each including a prologue before the camera turns to the sporting action. Like *Olympia*, the combined running time of both parts is approximately three hours with the majority of the first part dedicated to athletics. Other sports are montaged into the second part. Ichikawa also notably included multiple shots of spectators and judges alongside the focus on the athletes themselves and, much as Riefenstahl ensured that a camera focused on Hitler's reactions as a spectator, Ichikawa recorded the Japanese leader, Emperor Hirohito, both in attendance at, and enthused by, the Games. Like Riefenstahl, Ichikawa also found the *actualité* of the staged torch run visually ineffective and thus did not hesitate to restage the event from a more striking point of view.[18] Thus the dramatic footage of Mount Fuji forming the backdrop to a train-like entourage of runners passing diminutively in the foreground was specially orchestrated for the movie. Likewise, Ichikawa did not hesitate to ask athletes to re-enact certain scenes, or desist from editing footage from different races to give the impression of a single event. Finally, perhaps the most striking point of comparison between Ichikawa and Riefenstahl is both filmmakers' greater interest in the performance than the outcome. Like Riefenstahl, Ichikawa included extensive scenes of a given event without informing the spectator of the outcome. Furthermore, when results are given they are frequently mentioned in passing, and as far from being the most interesting aspect of what has just been witnessed. Yet despite these numerous borrowings, Ichikawa's film conveys a startlingly different message to that his predecessor. For where Riefenstahl sought to elevate the status of sportsperson to that of demi-god, Ichikawa set out more to bring his athletic *übermensch* back down to earth. Riefenstahl's athletes are perhaps best characterized by their sense of overall physical and mental control. Their abilities are thus presented as extraordinary, the product of highly trained, exceptional individuals. Ichikawa's, on the other hand, look anxious and uncertain. Here, in particular, Ichikawa exploited unobtrusive telephoto lenses to capture candidly the nervous ticks and momentary expressions of doubt revealed by the athletes in the moments immediately prior to, or following, the actual performance. In this way his film not only exposes the frailties and fallibility of the athletes, even at the moment of their greatest triumph, but also celebrates this is a sign of their greater humanity. In this way, Ichikawa later claimed that his film should be read as the very antithesis of Riefenstahl's.[19]

This very different mood is especially evident in the two prologues to *Tokyo Olympiad*. In the opening sequence, for example, the viewer is first confronted with a blood-red rising sun. Here the national metaphor is obvious to the point of overplay, and might be seen as echoing Riefenstahl's own emphasis on awakening in *Olympia*. However, far from giving way to hazy images referencing classical antiquity, Ichikawa then cuts to the very modern image of a bulldozer smashing through a building. The architectural emphasis of both films is thus retained, although the broken columns of antiquity in Reifenstahl's film are notably replaced with the post-war rebuilding of contemporary Japan. To reinforce further this explicitly post-war context, an aerial camera then hovers over the destroyed city of Hiroshima, while the commentary reminds the viewer of the destruction wrought thereupon. Ichikawa's acknowledgement of the classical origins of the Games is limited to a brief shot of the Olympic torch being lit in Greece. Even this rapidly transposes to images of the torchbearer taking a very different route to that adopted for the Berlin Games, as the various runners traverse the major cities of the Asian continent. Here it is not the classical past that Ichikawa evokes, but the very modern and internationalist history of the modern Olympic movement, as underscored by the commentator's potted history of the Games from 1896 to the then present day. Whereas Riefenstahl's film claimed an unbroken link between ancient Olympia and modern Berlin, Ichikawa proclaimed his continuity in terms of modern international sport, highlighting the arrival of Japan on the world stage.

'Balloons Over Hiroshima'; still from Ichikawa's *Tokyo Olympiad*.

'Ahamed Isa Under a Japanese Umbrella'; still from Ichikawa's *Tokyo Olympiad*.

It is, however, the prologue to the second part of Ichikawa's film that signals the most intriguing departure from Reifenstahl's *Olympia*. The sequence commences with a shot of a young, African athlete as he disembarks from an airliner beneath blinding floodlights. He is identified in the commentary as Ahamed Isa, an 800-metre runner from the former French colony of Chad, one of just two athletes from this new nation to have travelled to Tokyo. Isa is followed to the Olympic village where he is constantly shown looking bemused and overwhelmed by the whole spectacle of the Games. In a street scene, for example, he is presented as completely lost and in need of the guidance of a Japanese child. He is also shown sheltering beneath a Japanese umbrella, while the commentary suggests that this native of the desert regions of North Africa is not used to rain. And at the Olympic dining facilities he is shown eating alone, never mixing with the more boisterous European and North American athletes. When attention is focused on Isa's sporting contribution to the Games, it transpires that his prowess is far from exceptional. He is shown just once competing in a heat of the 800-metre race in which he fails to qualify for the next stage. Indeed, to emphasize the swiftness of his departure, shots of Isa running around the track are interspersed with shots of his marching around it during the opening ceremony. All this, of course, begs the question; why, precisely, does Ichikawa devote so much attention to this otherwise little noticed athlete? In one sense, Isa is presented as a visual metonym for all the participants in the Games: competitors, spectators, officials and media reporters alike. In a self-conscious rebuttal to the 'unity is strength' metaphor deployed by Riefenstahl in the prologue to the second part of *Olympia*, Ichikawa here privileges the mediocre athlete from a little known land over the triumphant, medal-winning national hero. Here, it seems, the true representative of the Olympic spirit is the individual lost in the crowd, rather than the standout performer taking all the plaudits. Ichikawa's more democratic, humanist focus can certainly be read as proposing an alternative to Riefenstahl's emphasis on authoritarian high-achievers. But it is not without its problems. The symbolic infantilization of Isa, for example, implies a problematic set of racial assumptions tied to long-rejected notions of evolutionary development. At the same time, the use of a mellow blues soundtrack to signify Isa's isolation collapses contemporary North African and urban American cultures, implying that they can be read as one and the same thing. None-theless, the symbolic implications of Ichikawa's focus on Isa would seem to be that a new world order is emerging, one in which both Africa and Asia will increasingly play a dominant role in international affairs. In the context of the Cold War politics of the 1960s, this was hardly an isolated notion, and suggests ways in which the Olympic Games, as a global spectacle, could both reflect and shape wider political and ideological debates in the second half of the twentieth century.

Other noteworthy filmmakers have also made contributions to the repertoire of Olympic films. Among these are: *13 jours en France*, a film recording events at the Grenoble winter Olympics in 1968 by the Cannes and Oscar winning director Claude Lelouch; and *O Sport, ty mir* (O Sport, You are the World), one of several documentaries made by the highly decorated Soviet film director Yuri Ozerov during the Moscow Games of 1980. Notably, Ichikawa, Lelouch and Ozerov also participated with other famous directors, including Milos Forman and John Schlesinger, on *Visions of Eight*, a compilation of eight short documentary films made by an interna-tional compendium of directors during the Munich Olympic Games of 1972.[20] While this latter produc-tion has drawn some critical attention, it has failed to attract the widespread approbation of its two iconic predecessors, perhaps not least because it is charged with having failed adequately to deal with the most notorious incident at the Munich Games, the Munich massacre in which eleven Israeli athletes and coaches were killed by members of the Black September terrorist organization.

The Olympic Games continue to provide a fasci-nating subject for documentary filmmakers. There can be little doubt, however, that Riefenstahl's *Olympia* and Ichikawa's *Tokyo Olympiad* occupy a position as the most exemplary interventions into the production of Olympic documentaries, while also remaining profoundly influential upon those who attempt to capture the Olympics on film.

five

THE RUSSIANS ARE COMING!
THE OLYMPICS AND THE COLD WAR

In July 1952 a contingent of more than 700 athletes, trainers and officials from the Soviet Union arrived in Helsinki to take part in the summer Olympic Games. For the local population, this minor 'invasion' must have triggered unhappy memories of a dozen years earlier, when Soviet troops had attacked Finland and bombed the capital during the so-called Winter War, the aftermath to the infamous Molotov–Ribbentrop Pact of 1939. This time, however, it was to be peaceful sporting competition, rather than military occupation, that determined the presence of the Soviet Union in the lands of its most northerly European neighbour. The impact made by the arrival of Soviet athletes in Helsinki was also felt more globally, not least because this was the first time that the communist state would take part in the Games. It was also abundantly clear that Soviet athletes were not there just to make up the numbers. Indeed, this inaugural appearance affirmed the Soviet Union's pre-eminent status on the world's sporting stage, as its athletes secured a total of 71 medals (22 golds, 30 silvers and 19 bronzes). Only the United States accrued more medals winning a total of 76 (40 golds, 19 silvers and 17 bronzes). From this point on, the Olympic Games would become one of the primary arenas in which the two post-war super-powers would wage battle for political and ideological supremacy. A new era in Olympic history was thus launched.

Spartacus versus Olympia

This was not the first time that a Russian presence had been felt at the Games. In the pre-revolutionary period, the former Tsarist Empire had sent teams of sportsmen to both the London (1908) and Stockholm (1912) Games. Here they picked up a handful of medals in figure skating, Greco-Roman wrestling and shooting events.[1] After 1917, however, the new Bolshevik regime expressly declared that it would not participate in what it openly described as a capitalist-inspired, bourgeois activity.[2] Instead, it set out to redefine sport in proletarian terms. While for some this meant the rejection of all sporting competitions, for others the primary objective was to establish an alternative organization to challenge the hegemony of the Olympic movement. Accordingly, in 1921 the Soviet authorities established a rival organization known as the Red Sport International (RSI) which staged its own international sporting events restricted to men and women from workers' organizations.[3] To distinguish its activities from its 'bourgeois' counter-part, the RSI designated its Games as Spartakiads, prioritizing the slave rebel of ancient Rome over the heroic athletes of classical Greece.[4] In practice, however, Spartakiads were virtually identical to Olympic Games. Both were multi-sport festivals featuring competitors from many nations, adopted

Да здравствует пролетарская Спартакиада в Москве!

'Long Live the Proletarian Spartakiad in Moscow!',
a cartoon published in *Izvestiya* (12 August 1928).

spectacle, typically in the form of a grand opening
ceremony as an integral aspect of proceedings, and
encouraged mass spectatorship. What distinguished
Spartakiads from their Olympic counterparts was the
explicit claim that these were political and ideological,
as well as sporting, events. Thus for the Soviet Union,
victory in sport was regarded as symptomatic of
far more than just successful individual or team
performances. Rather, or so the Soviet authorities
claimed, such victories reflected the superior conditions of socialism over capitalism. This concept was
notably articulated in visual terms in the official Soviet
press on the opening day of the first international

Spartakiad held in Moscow in 1928. On 12 August
the daily newspaper *Izvestiya* published a front-page
cartoon representing a Soviet sportsman dressed in
an amalgamation of sporting costumes to signify the
variety of activities – including swimming, athletics,
boxing, tennis and football – that made up the official
programme.[5] This veritable sporting giant towers over
a group of diminutive spectators, representatives of
the Western capitalist nations who had previously
dominated international sport. Envy and anxiety are
writ large on the faces of these spectators as they gaze
in awe at this new personification of Soviet proletarian
sport, about to crush all opposition before it.

The diversity and overt political affinities of Soviet
sport at the first international Spartakiad in 1928 were
also celebrated in a series of postcards designed by
the artist and photographer, Gustav Klutsis. In these
images, documentary photography was combined
with innovative typography to celebrate the collec-
tivity of sporting practice through the representation
of anonymous sportsmen and women, thus symbolizing all Soviet citizens. The inclusion of the Soviet
leader, Vladimir Ilych Lenin, in one of these images
adds an explicit political dimension to the works.
Stood astride the very mausoleum in Red Square
in which he was by this time buried, the father of
the new Soviet state has here seemingly risen from
the dead to express his explicit support for the
Spartakiad. Specially commissioned and produced
for widespread distribution both nationally and
internationally, these disposable representations of
the Soviet Union's alternative to the Western Olympic
Games have subsequently become collectors' items,
not least as key examples of the importance of sport
as a theme for major Soviet artists, and the development of Constructivism in the Soviet Union during
the 1920s.

Gustav Klutsis, *Postcard for the First Workers' Spartakiad*, 1928, lithograph.

Poster for the proposed but cancelled Workers' Spartakiad in Berlin in 1931.

Throughout the interwar years, the Soviet authorities retained a staunch opposition to the Olympic movement and continued to organize both national and international Spartakiads to counter the more dominant Western Games. In 1931, for example, the RSI planned to stage a second international Spartakiad, this time in Berlin. Political pressure, however, resulted in the German authorities cancelling the Games at the last minute.[6] Nonetheless, a poster had already been produced for the Games, suggesting the extent to which the RSI not only openly challenged the Olympic movement but also set out to use its rival international sporting festival as a rallying cry for political revolution. Here a physically robust athlete is represented astride a globe, his feet straddling the territory of the Soviet Union. Notably, he is shown with a hammer – a symbol of both sporting and labour practices – emblazoned with the letters RSI. As he swings this hammer, part tool, part sporting apparatus, miniscule figures representative of both the military and clerical authorities in France and Germany cower, or are swatted away like flies. Here the message was loud and clear. Participation in sporting events at the RSI-sponsored Spartakiad was far from a politically neutral gesture. Rather it was an explicit statement in support of the Soviet Union and an attack against the reactionary forces of conservatism, symbolized by the Olympic movement.

Leaping the Iron Curtain

It was not until the aftermath of the Second World War, as the geopolitical world order was transformed with the emergence of the Cold War, that the Olympic movement came to acquire a greater significance for the Soviet Union. Recognition of the vital role played by the Red Army in the Allied victory over National Socialist Germany had encouraged many Western nations now to welcome the Soviet Union into the international sporting community. In 1947, for example, the former Olympic gold medallist and IOC member Lord Burghley visited Moscow in an attempt to entice the former military allies to participate in the London Games of 1948.[7] This invitation, however, might be read as more than simply an altruistic gesture. Despite widespread anxieties concerning the state-sponsored, and thus non-amateur, status of many of the Soviet Union's top athletes, the IOC now recognized that the absence of the Soviet Union (and consequently the entire Eastern bloc) would be seriously detrimental to the internationalist credentials of the Games. At the same time, the Soviet authorities began to recognize the potential propaganda value of competing with, and hopefully defeating, the capitalist nations quite literally at their own game. Thus, despite the anti-internationalism of the immediate post-war campaigns launched in the Soviet Union, it was becoming increasingly clear that participation in the Olympic Games offered a unique political opportunity. Even the Soviet leader Iosif Stalin, never a great lover of sport, now moved towards supporting participation in the Olympic movement. For Stalin,

however, a guarantee of sporting success was a prerequisite.[8] In 1947, with little time for preparation, this looked unlikely and accordingly the Soviet Union decided not to send a team of athletes to London. It did, however, send a team of observers.[9] By 1951, the implementation of improved training programmes backed by state support meant that the chances of success were considerably enhanced. Having secured military victory on the battlefields of Europe the Soviet Union now sought to attain international supremacy on the world's sports fields. The Soviet Union was now ready to leave its mark on Olympic history.

The participation of the Soviet Union at the Helsinki Games certainly upped the ante as far as the world's media were concerned, making this Olympic festival one of the most widely reported to date. For the first time the Games were described as a 'battle of the giants' with competition between US and Soviet athletes dominating virtually all other concerns.[10] For the Western press, however, the presence of the Soviet team also posed more fundamental questions. What, for example, were the Soviet athletes actually like? How different were they to Western athletes and what effect had isolation from international sport had upon them? Were they really, as some had claimed, simply the product of an inhuman Soviet sports machine that was beginning to churn out high-performance athletes much as Soviet industry was fulfilling production demands for pig iron and steel? Or was this new, post-war generation more amenable to Western influence? Over the next few decades, competition between the ideologies of the communist and capitalist nations would take place on the playing fields of the Olympic Games. Visual representation, however, particularly as articulated in the mass media, would also provide an arena in which this ideological battle could be engaged. Here, a brief analysis of the various ways in which Soviet Olympic athletes were represented in the American press may offer some insights into the impact of Cold War thinking on the visual culture of the Games.

A Meeting of Minds and Bodies

During the Helsinki Games, athletes and officials from the major participating nations were housed in the official Olympic village at Käpylä, less than a mile and a half from the competition venues. Soviet athletes, as well as those from the Eastern European nations politically aligned with the Soviet Union (Bulgaria, Czechoslovakia, Hungary, Poland and Romania), took up alternative residence in temporary university accommodation at Otaniemi in the countryside surrounding the city.[11] This consciously implemented isolation was widely criticized by the Western media who immediately dubbed the site 'The Little Iron Curtain' village.[12] Possibly in response to this attack, the Soviet authorities altered this isolationist strategy and took steps towards encouraging, even celebrating, interactions between its athletes and those from the West. Thus, for example, *Time* magazine expressed some surprise when it reported:

> As the athletes began warming up for the first events, the big news was still the big Russian [sic] team (some 400 strong). Determinedly friendly from the first, they had made a point of visiting the US camp, chatting in sign language and translated wisecracks.[13]

Aptly capturing the mood of suspicion of the 'other' that typified much Cold War reportage at this time, the *Time* correspondent went on to suggest why such an unsolicited approach may have been adopted:

The Russians' [sic] own explanation for their strange behavior was the earnest assurance: 'We are here on a peace mission.' But some cynical observers, after hearing about Russian preparations for the games, thought they had hit on a better explanation. Last year alone, the USSR spent billions of rubles on its athletic program, skimmed off the top cream of some 25 million totally organized athletes for Helsinki. Apparently the Russians felt sure enough of their prospects to be able to afford a few smiles of anticipation.[14]

Despite the anxiety and disapproval elicited in the press, the interaction between US and Soviet athletes both on and off the field of play rapidly became a characteristic feature of the Helsinki Games and one that was widely reported, especially among the photo-journalistic fraternity.

One of the better-known reporters present in Helsinki was Ralph Crane, a staff photographer for *Life* magazine. Unlike many of his colleagues at the Games, Crane was not a sports photographer. His reputation lay in the photo-story, weaving simple narratives around a series of candid, seemingly unposed, shots that captured the 'essence' of a given moment or event. While in Helsinki, Crane rarely entered the stadium or other competition arena. Instead, he photographed athletes during their free time, gathering at canteens or chatting with each other at their respective Olympic bases. Clearly his primary objective was to capture images of US and Soviet athletes interacting with one another. At first glance, many of these images might be seen as exemplifying a mood of *détente*, providing incontrovertible evidence of the capacity of sport, and the Olympic Games in particular, to break down barriers and facilitate friendly dialogue between individuals

Ralph Crane, *American and Soviet Olympic Athletes, Helsinki, 1952.*

whose nationalities have, as an accident of history, constructed them as enemies. Here, the idea that sport enables communication across a political, ideological, and frequently linguistic, divide is seemingly celebrated and the oppositional stance of wider Cold War politics is thus undermined. Closer scrutiny of these works, however, can also reveal an underlying agenda that reinforces, rather than challenges, many of the Cold War anxieties and clichés inevitably generated by this friendly meeting of ideological enemies in the hotbed of Olympic competition.

A particularly striking example of this is a photograph by Crane representing four male athletes, two from the United States and two from the Soviet Union, seated on a bench beneath trees in what appears to be the Olympic Village at Käpylä. Here, while open dialogue is clearly taking place, it is notable that it is the more relaxed American sportsman who leads the conversation while the two Soviet athletes lean forward, listening intensely, and seemingly hanging on to his every word. The figure on the far right is so keen to be a part of this group that he perches, precariously, on the edge of the bench in what must be a most uncomfortable position. In contrast, the American athlete on the far left, occupies considerable space on the bench, but shows no willingness to adjust his position despite the obvious marginalization of his compositional counterpart. Though attached to the group, he seems far more reluctant to participate in this dialogue. Instead he stares down at his hands, physically and emotionally distancing himself from the Soviet athletes whom, it might be presumed, he regards as a little too close for comfort. The somewhat unconventional framing of this image is also striking. Confined in the lower left of the image, the American athletes seem crowded, obliged physically to defend their space. The verticality and outstretched left leg of the more centrally positioned American athlete here provides a clear physical buffer against the more dynamic lean of a metaphorical Soviet advance guard emerging from a birch forest. This image thus implies a very particular relationship between East and West. The American athletes, individuals to the core, express either engaged superiority or disengaged reluctance to communicate with their Soviet counterparts. The latter, on the other hand, show an unflagging fascination for the Americans, adding nothing to the discussion but eagerly consuming the 'wisdom' of the West. But does this signify a desire to embrace American ideals or slowly to encroach into the enemy's camp? Are these athletes symbolic of potential defectors or conniving invaders? Certainly both characteristics were the staple of Western stereotyping of Soviet citizens at this time.

Visual links between Soviet sport and militarism were also notably foregrounded in a series of *Life* magazine photographs published during the Games, taken by *Life* staff photographers, including Nat Farbman and Mark Kauffman. For example, the Soviet discus thrower Boris Matveev was captured in full

Boris Matveev ('Bushel Head Boris'), photograph from *Life* magazine (28 July 1952).

motion during a practice session. Here, however, rather than emphasizing the grace and rhythm of the spin conventionally deployed in representations of discus throwers, Matveev is shown grimacing and adopting a clumsy posture more reminiscent of a grenade thrower. The accompanying headline, 'How Reds "Mobilized"', only serves to reinforce the aggression and gracelessness of the Soviet athlete who is further demeaned in the caption describing him as 'Bushel-Head Boris' in reference to his swirling locks. Soviet women athletes fared little better. In the same issue, for example, shot-putter Tamara Tyshkevich is presented as 'Tank-Shaped

Tamara', alongside a headline reading 'To Win Olympic "War"'. Tyshkevich is notably represented at the precise moment at which she has fully released the shot. Her outstretched arm accordingly replicates a Nazi salute, a none-too-subtle reinforcement of the notion that all Soviet athletes might be seen as posing a threat to world peace. Even when Soviet athletes were represented in more sympathetic poses that emphasized dynamic sporting action, the message still seems dominated by Cold War anxieties. For example, an image of Soviet discus thrower, Nina Dumbadze, shows her performance being watched by American shot-putter Jim Fuchs. Here the explicitly voyeuristic context, implying that the American athlete might be more interested in

Nat Farbman, *Tamara Tyshkevich ('Tank-Shaped Tamara')*, photograph from *Life* magazine (28 July 1952).

Dumbadze's physique than her technique, is reinforced by the crude headline 'Muscles Pop through Iron Curtain'. Yet even in this context, suspicion seems to be as much aroused as libido, as Dumbadze is watched not only by the intrigued American athlete, but also a group of trench-coated, shadowy figures. Surveillance, here, is very much the watchword.

Man and Child: Western Constructions of Soviet Women Olympians

At the Helsinki Games, just over 10 per cent of the medals won by US athletes came in women's events. This was in notable contrast to the more than 30 per cent female medal winners for the Soviet Union, a remarkable achievement given that women competed in only 25 events compared to the 124 competitions for men. In athletics, regarded as the showcase event of the Games, the gender divide was even more stark. Thus of the 31 US medal winners, only one came in women's events, while almost two thirds of the Soviet medals (11 out of 17) were won by female athletes. Over the next two decades the performances of Soviet male athletes improved relative to their female counterparts, but women continued to dominate Soviet sporting achievements at the Olympic Games. Further, sportswomen from the Soviet Union's Eastern European satellite nations, including Czechoslovakia, the German Democratic Republic, Hungary, Poland and Romania, also achieved major Olympic successes during the next two decades. This certainly served the ideological objectives of the Soviet authorities as such victories were claimed as a reflection of greater gender equality under communism compared to Western capitalism. The response of Western nations to the sporting successes of Soviet Bloc women was here particularly striking. Certainly the propaganda potential associated

Mark Kauffman, *American Athlete Jim Fuchs Watches Soviet Discus Thrower Nina Dumbadze*, photographed above the caption 'Muscles Pop Through Iron Curtain' in *Life* magazine (28 July 1952).

with these international victories was recognized. However, the general trend in the West was less towards providing greater opportunities for its own sportswomen. Rather, the successes of Soviet Bloc sportswomen were increasingly presented as evidence not of superior sporting skill but of an 'aberrant socio-normativity'. Once again, visual culture would be used to back these dubious claims.

The most notable example of this came in the early 1960s with the victories of the Soviet athlete sisters Irina and Tamara Press. At the 1960 Olympic Games in Rome Tamara Press won a gold medal in the shot put competition and a silver in the discus. Four years later, in Tokyo, she followed this up with a double victory in both events. Irina, the younger of the sisters, proved victorious in the 80-metre hurdles in Rome and

doubled her tally of gold medals by winning the pentathlon in Tokyo. Unsurprisingly, the Press sisters were lauded as national heroines back in the Soviet Union. In the West, however, they were widely lambasted in the press. In 1960, for example, the *Los Angeles Times* described Tamara Press as resembling a 'blond lady piano-mover'.[15] Four years later the same newspaper, reporting on the 1964 Games, compared Press with American baseball legend 'Babe' Ruth.[16] This comparison was clearly intended to emphasis Ruth's weight and appearance far more than his skill. By now, however, what had started out as innuendo was beginning to give way to direct accusations that such victories could only have been achieved if the Press sisters were really men disguised as women. In popular reportage, the sisters were now

Tamara Press (left) *and Irina Press* (right), photographs from the *Life* magazine article 'Are Girl Athletes Really Girls?' (7 October 1966).

dubbed the Press brothers and in 1966, featured prominently in a now infamous *Life* magazine article entitled 'Are Girl Athletes Really Girls?'[17] The article was notably illustrated with photographs of the Press sisters, alongside other Soviet Bloc athletes, each captured at moments of extreme physical exertion. Here the tensed muscles and grimacing faces of the female athletes were presented as if such physical comportment somehow provided visual evidence of a dubious femininity. To contrast this notion of straining Soviet Bloc athletes, a comparative photograph of British athlete Mary Rand, Olympic victor in the 1964 women's long jump competition, was also included. Rand, however, was notably represented in a significantly more passive, even demure, pose set against a bucolic English landscape complete with church tower. Furthermore, she is shown carrying her four-year-old daughter, thus emphasizing her maternal status and implying that procreativity is thus a defining feature of femininity. The photographs in the *Life* article reinforced dominant Western gender conventions, articulating women as passive, submissive, lacking in physical strength and with maternal qualities, explicitly contrasted to a 'distorted' version of femininity purportedly evident in female athletes from the Soviet Bloc. The highly problematic claim here is that the success of Soviet and Eastern European female athletes was predicated not upon their superior sporting abilities, or the full support of their nations, but on a failure to adhere to conventional standards of gender normativity.

The *Life* magazine article was notably reporting on the first case of gender verification testing in international sport, carried out in September 1966 at the European Track and Field Championships in Budapest. Later that same year, the IOC announced that similar tests would be introduced for the Olympic Games of 1968, thus responding directly to the unsubstantiated claims made about the Press sisters and other Soviet Bloc athletes. In practice, this test proved highly controversial. Certainly the privacy and dignity of female athletes (no male athlete was ever asked to take such a test) was seriously compromised by the test that, in any case, proved to be highly ineffective. It is also worth noting here that no account was taken of any form of genetic variation or intersexuality.[18] Yet, despite protests from both sportswomen and significant sections of the scientific and medical community, gender verification testing continued throughout the remainder of the Cold War, only finally being abolished in the wake of the Atlanta Games of 1996.[19] It seems clear here that the emergence of gender verification testing at the Olympic Games was a specific Cold War response to the successes of Soviet Bloc female athletes in the 1950s and '60s. Although no such athlete ever failed the test, those who failed to participate in the programme – including the Press sisters who retired at the same time as the test was introduced – were subsequently damned by implication. Thus the reputations of Tamara and Irina Press remain to this day very much framed by questions of their gender identity.[20] As Ann Hall has argued, gender verification testing can be read as a form of 'body McCarthyism', an integral element within the wider Cold War battle defining communism itself as a 'deviant' form of socio-normativity.[21] In this context, not only women's sport but also the process of representing sportswomen in visual culture, as evidenced by the example of the carefully selected photographs published in *Life* magazine, became a key weapon in the ideological conflict of the Cold War.

Enter the Gymnasts

The success of Soviet sportswomen at the Olympic Games, however, was not confined solely to track and field events. Gymnastics had been practiced in Russia as early as 1830 and was introduced into school and college education in the 1870s.[22] Following the Bolshevik revolution, the sport retained its popularity, not least as a consequence of Lenin's well-documented claim that he practised gymnastics everyday while imprisoned or in exile.[23] Internationally, gymnastics was also one of the inaugural sports practised at the Olympic Games in Athens in 1896. Initially a team event, competitions for individual male gymnasts were introduced four years later at Paris in 1900, although women would be excluded from competition for the best part of another three decades. Female gymnasts did, however, participate in mass displays such as that staged during the Games of 1908 in London. In 1928 an all-round team event for women was introduced for the first time but this was dropped for the Los Angeles Games of 1932. In Berlin in 1936 and London in 1948 this was reintroduced, but it was not until the Helsinki Games of 1952 that women first competed in individual events. Gymnasts from the Soviet Union and Eastern Europe here proved utterly dominant. In the five individual competitions, the Soviet Union won three gold medals, five silvers and a bronze, while Hungary won the other two gold medals and four bronzes. In the all-round team event the Soviet Union were victorious with Hungary in second place. Czechoslovakia took the only remaining bronze medal. Over the next two decades the Soviet Union reaffirmed its dominance in women's gymnastics, securing the lion's share of the medals on offer. Thus when the Soviet women's team arrived in Munich in 1972 to compete in the Games, their success in the gymnastics arena never looked in doubt. What was not predicted, however, was the impact that one young performer would have not only on the Games themselves, but also on international relations in the Cold War.

Up to this point, gymnastics had very much been a sport for fully mature women. Thus the most successful gymnasts at the Helsinki Games, Nina Bocharova and Maria Gorokhovskaya, were aged 27 and 30 years respectively. Similarly, the most famous Soviet gymnast of this era, Larissa Latynina, notably won six medals, including two golds, at the Tokyo Olympics of 1964 at the age of 29. It would be another two years before she retired from competition. At the time of the Munich Games, Olga Korbut was just seventeen years old and the youngest member of the Soviet team but soon became the star of the show. Korbut was not, in fact, the most successful athlete at the Games of 1972. Her haul of three gold medals and one silver pales by comparison with US swimmer Mark Spitz's seven golds. Even Korbut's own teammate, Lyudmila Turisheva, secured as many medals as Korbut, though significantly fewer headlines.[24] Nor, indeed, was Korbut's performance the biggest story at the Games. The devastating events of the Munich massacre, in which eleven Israeli athletes were taken hostage and subsequently murdered by the terrorist Black September group, certainly put the Soviet gymnast's performances into a comparative perspective. Over the course of the Games, however, it was Korbut's image that would come to dominate the Western media, not least because her remarkable gymnastic abilities transformed the sport in which she excelled. Korbut was the first gymnast in competition to perform a backward somersault on the balance beam and a standing backward somersault on the asymmetric bars. She even had a move, the 'Korbut flip' named in her honour. But it was not just her gymnastic abilities that were celebrated. Korbut's charm, vulnerability and humanity, expressed through her unselfconscious smiles and tears, also drew significant media attention, as well as millions of television viewers across the globe.

Our Little Olga

Korbut's physical appearance and behaviour were a major factor in her rapid rise to global popularity. Her 'waif-like prepubescence', to quote Jan Graydon, enhanced by pigtails and seemingly unmediated emotional responses to the ups and downs of competition, served to accentuate a widely held notion that Korbut was not just a young athlete, but little more than a small child.[25] Certainly she was typically represented as much younger than her actual seventeen years in both text and image. Here, however, it is important not to lose sight of the fact that the Western media embrace of Korbut, and not least the wide dissemination of images of the Soviet gymnast, were similarly linked to a potential for political exploitation within the broader context of the Cold War. Korbut came to symbolize both political innocence and a new generation, and was thus distanced in the minds of Western spectators from what were regarded as the worst excesses of Soviet communism. The previous emphasis on the 'aberrant' gender identity in female Soviet athletes was now giving way to infantilization.

In March 1973, just six months after her success in Munich, Korbut and a team of Soviet women gymnasts travelled to the United States to take part in a coast-to-coast tour of seven major cities. Although more a display than a competitive event, the tour nonetheless attracted the attention of the pre-eminent sports publication in the United States, *Sports Illustrated*. In an article tellingly entitled 'Hello to a Russian Pixie', Martha Duffy, better known for her *Time* reports on

fashion and the visual arts, highlighted the extent to which the Western press revelled in representing Korbut in the guise of a small child. This 'elfin Russian girl', wrote Duffy, 'the girl of tears and triumph at the Olympics' had a smile that 'drew the kind of reaction that only a 6-month-old baby can usually manage'. But it was not just Korbut's appearance that was shaped by Duffy's imagination. She also stereotyped the Soviet gymnast's behaviour, constructing an image of Korbut as a mildly rebellious child familiar to Western parents. Thus she is described as the ringleader in horseplay among the 'girls' and carries with her an unconventional stuffed toy, a hedgehog with hair the colour of violet and a smell of candy. Along with the other gymnasts, she rises at 6.30 a.m. to watch cartoons on the television and loves tomato ketchup.[26] Despite appearing in a dedicated sports magazine, the article barely mentions Korbut's gymnastic abilities.

A photograph of Korbut was also notably included on the cover of the issue in which Duffy's article appeared. Here, Korbut is shown adopting a pose during one of her performances. Her twisted torso notably serves specifically to emphasis her immature body, flattening any evidence of breasts and straightening her hips. Further, her stretched neck and raised chin recalls the kind of posture frequently adopted by small children when trying to look taller and more grown-up. Even the accompanying caption, 'From Russia with Charm', subverts the more adult associations with the familiar title of Ian Fleming's Cold War spy novel of 1957 (and film of 1963), replacing the sexual allusion of the original with one suggestive of a more innocent admiration.

By the time of the US tour, Korbut was already being presented as an international celebrity in the Western press. By the end of 1972 she had been awarded the BBC Overseas Sports Personality of the

FROM RUSSIA WITH CHARM

Olga Korbut Tours the U.S.

Olga Korbut on the cover of *Sports Illustrated* magazine (10 March 1973).

Gymnast Olga Korbut Holding Her Gold Medal at the 1972 Munich Olympic Games.

Year and the Associated Press Female Athlete of the Year (the only Soviet athlete ever to win this award). Back in Moscow she became the youngest recipient of the title Honoured Master of Sport in gymnastics. In Britain she was introduced to both the Queen and Prime Minister Edward Heath, and in the United States had a much-publicized encounter with President Richard Nixon at the White House.[27] She was also famously photographed with Mickey Mouse. Korbut's growing celebrity status in the West certainly reflected a change in the wind. In the United States, for example, the Soviet gymnast was increasingly embraced not only in the guise of a child, but also as 'one of our own'. As Duffy reported, at Houston Airport all the Soviet gymnasts were presented with Stetsons, a clear symbol of Texan, and by extension American, culture. While all the girls delightedly accepted this gift, they revealed their status as outsiders by wearing the hats clumsily. Indeed, 'only Olga gets the right angle', Duffy reported, 'straight down almost to the eyes'.[28] A photograph published in the journal seemingly sought to confirm this claim to millinery allegiance.

All Grown Up

As things turned out, Korbut's celebrity status in the West was heavily dependent upon the infantilization of her image. In this guise her communist affiliations seemed not only diminished, but she could also be read as a reflection of the possibility of change in the Soviet Union itself. Indeed her appearance on the world stage could hardly have been better timed. Just weeks before the Munich Games began, the first Strategic Arms Limitation Treaty (SALT I) had been signed, ushering in a new era of collaboration between East and West. In this context, the gymnast was later tellingly described by sportswriter Leigh Montville as '85 pounds of pigtailed détente'.[29] Korbut thus offered a very different image of the Soviet sportswoman than the previous dominant stereotype of the muscular, militarized and masculinized athlete. The mischievous, yet charming, child simultaneously seemed more appealing and less threatening. The problem, however, was precisely the fact that Korbut's childlike image could not be retained indefinitely.

In 1976 Korbut appeared at the Montreal Games to defend her titles. Although still only 21 years old at this time, she was already losing the support of an international public that had loved her just a few years earlier. No longer cheered for her every gesture, she was increasingly described as past her best, 'washed out and washed up'.[30] The new star of the show, notably, was an even younger gymnast, fourteen-year-old Romanian Nadia Comaneci, who outstripped Korbut's previous Olympic achievement by winning three gold medals, one silver and one bronze. Nor was it just in the gymnastics arena that Comaneci usurped Korbut's position. Now she also replaced Korbut in the hearts and minds of Western spectators as well as on the covers of major Western journals. Comaneci's status, as being even younger than Korbut in her prime, secured her perceived position as a political neutral, a replacement for Korbut whose broad exploitation by the Soviet authorities now threatened her popular identity as a political innocent. Moreover, as John MacAloon has argued, Romanian national identity reinforced the notion of Comaneci as 'a political captive of the Soviets', and thus a Cold War victim to be supported in the West. Korbut's reign as a successful Soviet gymnast turned out to be as short-lived as her youth. Her popular image as a Western celebrity, however, was dependent less on her athletic abilities than on the role her image played within the context of Cold War *détente* in the 1970s.

By the end of the decade, this popular, if mythically constructed, image of a charming, childlike Soviet athlete who potentially made the world momentarily forget its troubles, began to lose both its appeal and its relevance as political tensions between East and West began to ratchet up once more. The age of the 'innocent' had well and truly passed.

We're Not Playing Anymore

In December 1979 Soviet troops invaded Afghanistan, thus bringing the period of international *détente* to a crashing halt. As Cold War relations between East and West sunk to a new low, the question of what role the Olympic Games would now play in international diplomacy became more pressing than ever, not least because the next Games were scheduled to take place the following year in Moscow. To add further political spice to this circumstance, Moscow had been awarded the Games in preference to its only rival, Los Angeles. For US President Jimmy Carter, the Moscow Games had the potential to act as a bargaining chip in international diplomacy. Thus, in February 1980 the United States threatened to boycott the Games unless Soviet troops withdrew from Afghanistan. By March, less than four months before the scheduled opening ceremony, Carter not only confirmed the boycott but also called upon other nations to follow so that when the Games commenced, the absence not only of US athletes, but also of those from 64 other nations, seriously diminished the 'internationalism' of the Olympic festival. Four years later, the Soviet Union and thirteen other nations reciprocated the boycott by withdrawing from the Games of 1984, held in Los Angeles. Whereas previously the Olympic Games had provided an arena in which the two Cold War superpowers would compete against each other, now the competition, it

seemed, was specifically focused upon not competing. By 1988, when both nations again agreed to participate at the Seoul Games, the Cold War was already entering its swan-song era. Economic crises in the Soviet Union had necessitated major reforms that, in turn, would lead to the final collapse of the communist regime. Thus, a year before the Barcelona Games were due to commence, events in Moscow precipitated a crisis that would eventually lead to the dissolution of the Soviet Union.

The collapse of the Soviet political system ultimately resulted in the former state being broken up into its constituent nations. As a consequence of this, the three Baltic Republics (Estonia, Latvia and Lithuania) formed their own National Olympic Committees (NOCs) in 1991, and have competed independently at subsequent Olympic Games. In 1992, however, the other twelve former Soviet nations (Armenia, Azerbaijan, Belarus, Georgia, Kazakhstan, Kyrgyzstan, Moldova, Russia, Tajikistan, Turkmenistan, Ukraine and Uzbekistan) not only participated in Barcelona as a Unified Team, but also topped the overall medal table. Thus the international success of Soviet sport still hung like a spectre over the Games even after the Soviet Union itself no longer existed. A year later, these nations finally formed their own NOCs and now compete as independent states.

The end of the Cold War brought about the end of the Olympic Games as a metaphorical battleground between the two superpowers. By 1996, Russia was falling some distance behind the United States in the overall medal table, and both in 2004 and 2008 would also finish behind China. In the post-Cold War era, a new world order in international Olympic sport has already emerged. Ultimately, the Cold War defined the Olympic Games throughout much of the later twentieth century, transforming not only the Olympic movement as a whole but also the broader

Nadia Comaneci on the cover of *Sports Illustrated* magazine (17 July 1976).

meanings ascribed both to sport itself and to those who participated in sport. And it was not just the performances of the athletes that contributed to these shifts in meaning. The various ways that both male and female Soviet athletes were represented in the Western press also exposes the underlying tensions, anxieties and prejudices that shaped broader understandings of what Olympic participation might signify. Whether imaged as dangerous components within a vast, inhuman Soviet sports machine or youthful individuals likely to seek political refuge in the West, as super-muscled, masculinized women or innocent, cutesy child-performers, the political tensions between East and West shaped these conventionalized identities and constructed personalities, and thus the broader image, of the Olympic Games at this crucial moment in history.

With the Soviet era rapidly becoming a distant memory, the broader historical representation of Soviet sport at the Olympic Games is also now undergoing something of a transformation. In 2003, for example, the Russian artist Grisha Bruskin produced a series of plaster sculptures under the collective title 'Archaeologist's Collection'. Among the works forming this collection is a torso of a Soviet athlete, wearing a sports costume adorned with the letters CCCP (USSR). The fragmented form of Bruskin's miniature monument clearly alludes to iconoclasm, referencing the widespread acts of vandalism perpetrated upon symbols dedicated to the former Soviet regime in the aftermath of its overthrow. In this context, the work might be read as an abandoned relic of a long-past era. Here the suggestion of violence perpetrated against this object seems to stand metaphorically for an explicit rejection of the values associated with that very regime, especially as articulated through the figure of the sportsman. But, might there not perhaps be a degree of ambiguity at play? After all, in cultural terms, the fragmented sculptural torso also calls to mind the classical tradition. And in this context, might Bruskin's work not also open itself to positive readings of nostalgia for a past heroic era, one in which victory in the international sporting arena, particularly at the Olympic Games, played a vital role? Bruskin's fragmentary figure, as part of a series of works that overtly refer to archaeological discovery, notably entered the public arena at a time when post-Soviet society was itself undergoing a reassessment and re-evaluation of its Soviet past. Here such discourses frequently focused upon the legacy of the Soviet past and posed the question: Should the collapse of the authoritarian Soviet state ultimately be celebrated or mourned?[31] Bruskin's *Athlete* speaks eloquently to this issue, while steadfastly refusing to provide an answer.

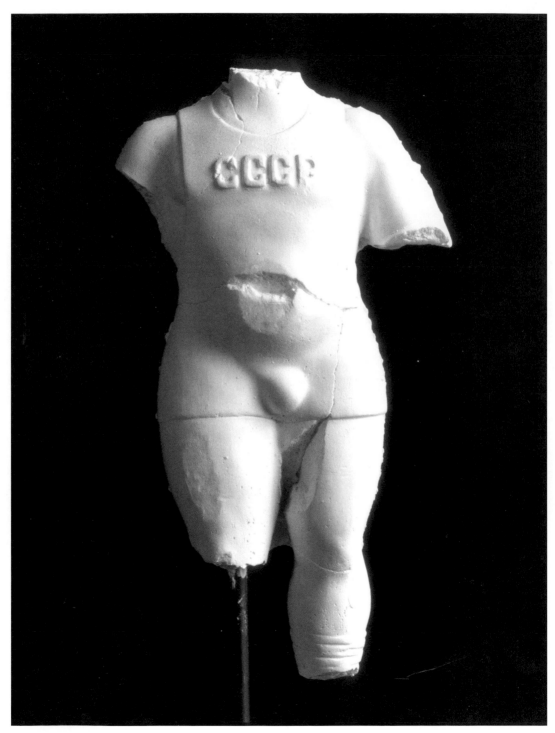

Grisha Bruskin, *Athlete*, from the series *Archaeologist's Collection*, 2003, painted bronze.

Ben Johnson Winning the 100-metres Final at the 1988 Seoul Olympic Games.

six

OLYMPIC TRANSGRESSIONS: DRUGS, POLITICAL PROTEST AND TERRORISM

Participation in Olympic competition has often been characterized as the idealistic pursuit of honour and glory over material reward, a concept conventionally traced back to the ancient Games where the only prize offered was a symbolic olive wreath. Nonetheless, even at Olympia success frequently brought economic, as well as symbolic, benefit. For example, on return to his home state, a victorious athlete was frequently inundated with lavish gifts, ranging from cash prizes to free services for a lifetime.[1] Thus sporting success, and its consequent fame, was widely understood to attract fortune as much in ancient times as it does in the modern era. Perhaps inevitably, this generated a willingness among some athletes to transgress both convention and rule in order to secure such victories. Accordingly, controversy and scandal regularly cast a shadow over ancient Olympia. Pausanias, for example, cites several cases of bribery and corruption among competitors, including boxers, pentathletes and wrestlers, from Eupolos of Thessaly in the fourth century BC to Damonikos of Elis, nearly 400 years later.[2] When exposed, such dishonesty was, of course, roundly condemned. Regarded as a sleight both against the gods and fellow competitors, the guilty were described as having brought shame upon themselves and their native regions. They were also forced to pay fines for their misdemeanours, with the funds

raised used to erect statues dedicated to Zeus, known as the Zanes. Though these statues are no longer in existence, they are believed to have represented the God hurling his thunderbolt in anger. The pedestals, which can still be seen at Olympia, carried stern inscriptions declaring that honest performance only, and not cash, would win eternal glory.[3] Lining the entrance to the stadium, these statues reinforced the condemnation of such transgressions, while simultaneously acting as visual deterrents, timely reminders to all athletes not only of the demand for fair play, but also of the dishonour that failure to conform to this would inevitably bring.[4] It might be added in hindsight, however, that as the cases of corruption cited by Pausanias range across several centuries, the overall efficacy of the Zanes might perhaps be questioned.

Cheating, of course, was hardly restricted to ancient times. Following the model established at Olympia, the Games of the modern era similarly offered little other than symbolic reward, although a medal, as well as an olive branch was conferred on the victorious. Similarly, however, such successes could bring other rewards in kind, as the victory of Louis Spiridon in the first Olympic marathon had shown. One notorious early example of transgressing both the regulations and the spirit of the Games occurred during the marathon at St Louis in 1904. As the author of the Official Report, Charles J. P. Lucas, recounted:

> There are many brilliant and happy incidents connected with the Marathon races held both in Athens and at Paris, and so, too, there should have been in America, but indeed, the brilliant finale of a great race, of the greatest honor ever brought to American shores by an American athlete was robbed of its lustre, when Fred Lorz, of the Mohawk Athletic Club, New York, after riding a number of miles in an automobile . . . ran the last five miles of the Marathon race, covered the last 440 yards of the 24 miles and 1500 yards in the Stadium, and was hailed like a conquering hero by the American people.[5]

Lorz's 'assisted victory' was, of course, immediately annulled. This, however, did not restrain Lucas from issuing a vociferous condemnation of such un-gentlemanly behaviour, declaring 'the perfidy of Lorz will never be forgotten'.[6]

Enhanced Performances

Given this self-righteous tone, Lucas's subsequent description of the means by which the rightful winner of the race, Thomas J. Hicks, achieved victory, may strike the modern reader as somewhat surprising. As Lucas continued, Hicks 'was running the last ounces of strength out of his body, kept in mechanical action by the use of drugs, that he might bring to America the Marathon honors, which American athletes had failed to win both at Athens and at Paris'.[7] Indeed Lucas willingly described how he himself was part of the team that had administered sulphate of strychnine to the athlete seven miles out from the finishing line. Shortly after this, as the athlete again showed signs of flagging, Hicks was given a second dose of strychnine. Subsequently he 'appeared to revive' and began 'running mechanically like a well-oiled piece of machinery'.[8] It should be noted, of course, that neither Hicks nor Lucas, unlike Lorz, were in any way transgressing the rules of the competition. At this time there were no regulations banning competitors from using any substances whatsoever to enhance their performances. Indeed, Lucas was proud of his

Thomas Hicks Being Assisted During the 1904 St Louis Olympic Games.

'Dorando [Pietri], of Italy, being helped across the finish line in the marathon, which later disqualified him', at the 1908 London Olympic Games.

contribution to this victory, pointing out that 'Hicks was far from being the best man physically in the race' and that the fundamental difference between Hicks and his opponents lay in Lucas's own judicious application of drugs.[9] Lucas further claimed that, 'the Marathon race, from a medical standpoint, demonstrated that drugs are of much benefit to athletes along the road'.[10] Four years later, at the London Games of 1908, Italian marathon runner Dorando Pietri became perhaps the most famous athlete ever to be disqualified from Olympic competition. His misdemeanour, however, was not the fact that he too had taken strychnine to aid his performance but that, against his will, he had been assisted over the finishing line after collapsing.

The use of nutritional or pharmaceutical substances to enhance sporting performance probably dates back to ancient times. As Judith Swaddling has pointed out, mood and behaviour altering herbal medications were widely known and freely available in the ancient world and, while there is no evidence to confirm the specific use of drugs at the ancient Games, it seems likely that athletes would willingly have taken substances believed to be beneficial.[11] As Lucas's account suggests, the revival of the Games provided a context in which modern athletes began to look to medical supplements as a means to gain an advantage over their opponents. The development of synthetic steroids in the 1930s, and the increased use of amphetamines at about the same time, certainly changed the landscape as far as the possibilities for the use of performance-enhancing drugs were concerned, although there is little concrete evidence to suggest when these may first have been used in a sporting context. It was not until the death of the Danish cyclist, Knud Enemark Jensen at the Olympic Games in Rome in 1960, however, that the issue of drug use at the Games began to attract widespread attention. Tragically, Jensen died after collapsing during the road race, thus becoming only the second Olympic athlete to die in competition during the modern era.[12] An official autopsy subsequently determined that the cause of death was the extreme temperature on the day of the race, though it also revealed traces of amphetamine in Jensen's body.

It was in the hothouse of international competition during the Cold War that the widespread use of drugs, and the issue of controlling their use, came to the top of the Olympic agenda. At this time claims were increasingly being made that athletes from communist nations were routinely using steroids. Although such claims were typically unsubstantiated, the spectre of widespread steroid use, as Rob Beamish and Ian Ritchie have pointed out, became synonymous with Cold War anxieties of communists making an 'unprincipled use of science to further political goals without apparent concern for human consequences'.[13] In this context, many feared that 'the Olympic Games would become the most visible and public site of extended chemical warfare between nation states'.[14] By 1967, the IOC followed the lead of other international sports federations and introduced a ban on all performance-enhancing drugs. Tests to detect such illegal substances were thus first used at the Games in Mexico City in 1968, since when over 100 athletes have tested positive for a variety of drugs from caffeine and codeine to anabolic steroids. Another fourteen cases of positive

drug tests have been detected at the winter Games between 1968 and 2010. Of all the athletes who have been identified as drug cheats, however, perhaps none has been as vilified as the Jamaican-born, Canadian sprinter Ben Johnson.

From Hero to Zero

The 100-metre final at the Seoul Olympic Games in 1988 was certainly one of the most anticipated sprint races of the late twentieth century. Here Johnson faced his archrival Carl Lewis, winner of four Olympic gold medals at the previous Games in Los Angeles. In the years prior to the Seoul Games, Lewis and Johnson had battled for the position as world's number one sprinter with Johnson beating Lewis on several occasions. It was the Olympic sprint final, however, that was widely regarded as the ultimate test that would prove which of the two athletes would reign supreme. When Johnson crossed the line in a new world-record time of 9.79 seconds, photographs of his victory were beamed across the world. Notoriously, Johnson not only defeated his opponent, but had the time, and the audacity, to look across the track and raise his arm in a victory salute while crossing the line. With the gold medal secured, Johnson could now further cash in on his fame and status as the world's fastest athlete. Within 72 hours, however, Johnson's world fell apart as news broke that he had tested positive for steroid use. Overnight the Canadian athlete's reputation went from all-conquering hero to villain in the mass media. In his native Ontario, for example, earlier images of a victorious Johnson, bedecked in a Canadian athletics vest, were replaced on the cover of the *Toronto Sun* with a photograph of a frowning, tight-lipped Johnson now shown wearing a patterned shirt more reminiscent of his Jamaican heritage.[15] Here, beneath the headline

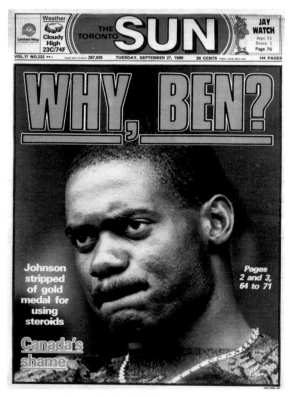

'Why, Ben?' Ben Johnson on the cover of the *Toronto Sun* (26 September 1988).

'Why, Ben?' and the caption 'Canada's Shame', Johnson is visually distanced not only from his sporting victory but also from his national affiliation. Notably, five years later, when Johnson was again caught using drugs, the Canadian Federal amateur sport minister Pierre Cadieux, reportedly expressed his disgust at Johnson by even suggesting that the athlete move back to Jamaica.

Since the Seoul Olympic Games, Johnson's image has been widely used as a signifier for the wider practice of drug cheating. It might be added here that Johnson's own post-1988 activities can hardly be said to have helped the rehabilitation of his public persona. In 1999, for example, Johnson became embroiled in a media scandal when it was reported that he had acted as a sports coach to Al-Saadi Gaddafi, son of the former Libyan leader. When Gaddafi subsequently signed for Italian Serie A football team Perugia in 2003, the fact that he failed a drugs test after his first match was widely reported. There is, of course, no evidence to suggest that Johnson was in any way associated with the younger Gaddafi's use of drugs, but the media were not slow to highlight the links between the two sportsmen, renowned for having tested positive for the use of performance-enhancing substances. In 2006 Johnson also appeared in a series of American television advertisements for an energy drink called Cheetah Power Surge. Here Johnson exploited his Olympic notoriety by ironically engaging in a conversation with Frank D'Angelo, president and CEO of the Toronto-based company that distributes the drink. 'Ben, when you run, do you Cheetah?', D'Angelo asks. 'Absolutely. I Cheetah all the time', Johnson replies before holding up a can of the energy drink for the camera. Given the media treatment he has received, whether deserved or not, Johnson perhaps cannot be blamed for exploiting his already shattered image in such a way. Yet what is most striking here is the longevity of Johnson's pre-eminence as a symbol the Seoul scandal, Johnson's image is probably still the most notorious and familiar of the numerous sportsmen and women found transgressing the rules at the Olympic Games. Like those athletes recorded by Pausanias as having cheated at the ancient Games, Johnson's current reputation remains shaped by this status while his image is often used as a warning to other athletes against the consequences of such actions. In this respect, the public image of Ben Johnson, in the modern media-driven era, is perhaps not dissimilar to that of the Zanes at ancient Olympia.

The Olympics and Race

Johnson's Canadian-Jamaican national identity, and the ease with which some sections of the media shifted the emphasis from the former to the latter once his drug use was uncovered, can be read as one episode within the wider context of race and discrimination at the Olympic Games. Today, the Olympic movement prides itself on its promotion of equal rights and racial integration and has enshrined non-discriminatory practices within the official Olympic Charter. The most recent edition of this, in effect since February 2010, cites as Fundamental Principle 5 that: 'Any form of discrimination with regard to a country or a person on grounds of race, religion, politics, gender or otherwise is incompatible with belonging to the Olympic movement.'[16] While such an aim is, of course, laudable, the history of the Games themselves reveals that transgressions against the basic principle of equal treatment for all races were much in evidence at earlier moments in Olympic history.

Although not every competitor at the first revived Games of 1896 has been definitively identified, it is likely that all were of European origin. The first non-white athlete recorded as competing at the Games was Constantin Henriquez de Zubiera, a Haitian-born member of the victorious French Rugby Union squad at the Paris Olympics of 1900.[17] Four years later at St Louis, two African runners, Len Tau and Jan Mashiani, competed alongside the Native American, Frank Pierce in the marathon.[18] Also in 1904, George Poage became the first African-American athlete to participate in the Games, securing bronze medals both in the 200-metre and 400-metre hurdles. Poage's success, however, far from reflected an enlightened attitude towards race at the Games of 1904. Certainly the segregation of spectators was still very much the order of the day at St Louis, though even this pales

into insignificance when compared with one of the most notorious events ever staged in conjunction with an Olympic festival.

In August 1904, in the midst of Olympic competitions and as part of the wider Louisiana Purchase Exhibition, spectators at the St Louis Games were invited to attend an event dubbed 'Anthropology Days'. This was billed as the world's first athletic competition exclusively for, in the words of the brainchild behind the event, James E. Sullivan, 'the several savage tribes' in attendance at the fair.[19] Continuing a pattern established at previous World's Fairs, the Louisiana Purchase Exhibition has gained much historical notoriety for its extensive displays of peoples from non-Western regions and cultures as a form of public spectacle. These so-called living exhibits inhabited 'authentic' reconstructed village settings, and were asked to perform cultural activities regarded as typical of 'primitive' societies. Widely condemned both at the time and subsequently, these displays were primarily designed to provide somewhat spurious evidence for the relative evolutionary advancement of Western civilization and the 'superiority' of the white race. For example, in a report published in January 1905 in *Spalding's Official Athletic Almanac*, Sullivan explicitly declared that the athletic events at the Anthropology Days were specifically intended as a riposte to 'the startling rumors and statements that were made in relation to the speed, stamina and strength of each and every particular tribe that was represented at St Louis'.[20] Though introduced as an anthropological and scientific experiment to test the athletic propensity of the different races, the Anthropology Days were in fact little more than a sham. In effect, a handful of randomly chosen non-white individuals were called upon to perform athletic activities, the vast majority without having had any previous experience of such sports and frequently showing little interest in participation. When, unsurprisingly, this group failed to attain levels of performance similar to those achieved by highly trained, specialist white athletes, Sullivan presented this data as incontrovertible evidence of the inferiority of all non-white races. By describing the sporting achievements of this hastily gathered and under-prepared group of athletes variously as 'very poor', 'very disappointing' and even 'ridiculously poor', Sullivan explicitly sought to scotch, once and for all, contemporary reports that advocated 'the natural athletic ability of the savage'.[21] His objective was to ensure the white man's place well and truly at the apex of his personally constructed model of racially determined sporting superiority.

Notably, visual imagery was an integral element within Sullivan's report, deployed to reinforce his con-troversial views. For example, of the nine photographs recording events at the Anthropology Days, three focus on the javelin competition, despite the fact that this was but one of sixteen events. While throwing the javelin had been a popular event in the pentathlon

at the ancient Olympic Games, the competition was not introduced into the modern Games until 1908, four year after St Louis. Moreover, the javelin used at the Anthropology Days scarcely resembled the slender sporting equipment presumed to have been used in ancient times and that would soon be introduced at the London Games. Rather the implement wielded at St Louis was, in effect, a tribal spear with a broad arrowhead, thus resembling the weapons convention-ally associated with African tribesmen as represented in populist and colonialist literature and imagery. Since the competitors at the Anthropology Days were also typically dressed in native costume, the clear distinction between the Western sportsman and Sullivan's conception of 'the savage' was thus visually reinforced. More importantly, perhaps, the images included in the report privilege what might be described as awkward postures, seemingly designed to show discomfort and a lack of physical harmony in the so-called native performers, especially when compared with the pictorial conventions typically used for Western athletes in other images throughout the report. For example, in an image captioned 'A Negrito

'Moro Throwing the Javelin', from *Spalding's Official Athletic Almanac for 1905: Special Olympic Number, Containing the Official Report of the Olympic Games of 1904.*

'Negrito from the Philippines in the Archery Contest', from *Spalding's Official Athletic Almanac for 1905: Special Olympic Number, Containing the Official Report of the Olympic Games of 1904.*

Archery Shooting', a young man is represented with a twisted back and bent knees as he is about to release his arrow. Alongside this young archer is a fellow African squatting on his haunches and perched precariously on a plank of wood. In the background, a man wearing a blazer and boater – presumably a judge – also crouches, but adopts a more upright posture as he inspects the actions of the competitors from a safe distance. Indeed isolation is here further emphasized by the distance between the athletes and the few spectators occupying the stands. Even the women at the very front of the stand are positioned behind a rail, a defensive barrier separating the space between spectator and the foreground competitors. It is also noteworthy, here, that the majority of the images representing the Anthropology Days make a point of including white spectators, usually officials, within the compositional frame. These figures thus operate both as representatives of authority and as surrogate viewers for the presumed audience of the photographs in the report: specifically the white community. The sporting action is thus defined as performed for the benefit of this latter social group and not the athletes themselves. To diminish further the significance of the performers, the athletes are usually identified in the accompanying caption not by their name (as are the white athletes in the report) but by their racial group.

The endemic racism, as explicitly articulated both in the organization of the Anthropology Days, and the officially published conclusions drawn from this absurd event have subsequently proved something of an embarrassment, not least to Olympic historians. Allen Guttmann, to quote just one commentator, has described the whole episode as nothing less than a 'disgrace'.[22] Even Coubertin, rarely celebrated for his enlightened views, condemned the Anthropology Days as 'particularly embarrassing' and an 'outrageous charade'.[23] While the Anthropology Days at the St Louis Olympics of 1904 certainly constitute one of the most shocking cases of abusing the Games to express profoundly problematic racial theories, this was far from being the last time that race would emerge as a central issue at the Olympic Games.

Two Myths, a Film and a Photograph

James Cleveland ('Jesse') Owens remains, perhaps, the most famous African-American Olympian of all time.

His four gold medal victories (100 metres, 200 metres, 4 x 100 metres and long jump) at the Berlin Olympic Games of 1936 stood alone as an athletic achievement (until matched in 1984 by Carl Lewis) and, since his death in 1980, Owens's achievements have been celebrated with the award of a posthumous Congressional Gold Medal, a national athletics prize named in his honour and a park and monument dedicated to his memory in his hometown of Oakville, Alabama. Images of Owens's victories in Berlin have also entered the public consciousness not only as a reflection of his extraordinary athletic prowess, but also as a symbol of resistance against the rise of Fascism in the 1930s. In this context, the success of the African-American athlete is recorded as a direct assault against Adolf Hitler's Aryan supremacy ideology and the National Socialist regime's political exploitation of the Olympic Games. Given the vast historical significance thus ascribed to Owens's sporting achievements, it is hardly surprising that a number of myths have come to define the meaning of events in Berlin in the summer of 1936. First, the notion that Hitler personally snubbed Owens, refusing to congratulate the African-American athlete after his victory in the 100-metre final, has persistently been reported in accounts of the Berlin Games.[24] However, after Hitler had congratulated some German athletes on his first day in attendance, he was advised not to proceed with this practice. After this point, the German leader offered his congratulations to no other athlete, German, African-American or otherwise. The second myth concerns Owens's closest competitor in the long jump, Luz Long of Germany. In 1964, nearly three decades after the event, Owens reported that Long had been instrumental in ensuring his own qualification for the final of the competition. During the qualifying round, Owens had just one jump remaining and, at this point, Long advised him

Luz Long and Jesse Owens at the 1936 Berlin Olympic Games.

to move his starting position back to guarantee a legitimate jump (Owens was easily more than capable of jumping the required distance). Thus the German athlete not only displayed the kind of fairness idealistically, if not always practically, associated with Olympism, but also revealed a rejection of the racism so embodied within National Socialism. The same year that Owens told this story, Long was posthumously awarded the Pierre de Coubertin Medal, also known as the True Spirit of Sportsmanship Medal (Long was killed in action in 1943). The authenticity of Owens's version of events has since been questioned although Long's goodwill, at the very least, remains much in evidence in the visual records of the Games.[25] In

Reifenstahl's *Olympia*, for example, Long is shown running enthusiastically to congratulate his opponent immediately after Owens's victorious jump knocked the German into second place. That Long was willing to show such an open expression of support for an African-American athlete in such a public arena is certainly testament to the humanity of the German athlete. It may also suggest the extent to which Owens's success in Berlin was far from unappreciated among a wider German population at the time. Furthermore, Owens and Long posed together for a series of photographs at the stadium, probably shortly after the competition. In all these photographs, Long and Owens are shown lying on their stomachs on the ground. Their faces remain close together and the amiability between the two competitors is much in evidence. In one of the photographs both athletes are shown breaking into a broad laugh as they clearly share a joke. Whether or not Owens's verbal account of the prelude to this encounter is fully accurate or not, the visual evidence clearly reveals genuine warmth between the African-American athlete and his National Socialist opponent. Indeed Owens would later state of Long: 'It took a lot of courage for him to befriend me in front of Hitler . . . You can melt down all the medals and cups I have and they wouldn't be a plating on the twenty-four carat friendship that I felt for Luz Long at

that moment.'[26] Though not widely distributed at the time of the Olympic Games of 1936, these images of Owens and Long sharing a joke offer a stark contrast to the official victory podium photograph in which Owens's military-style salute is countered by Long's raised right arm, the official Nazi gesture made mandatory for all German citizens in a decree of 1933. Owens's victories in Berlin were certainly great individual achievements and operated, at a symbolic level, as a rigorous challenge to the naked racism of National Socialist ideology, even if some of the myths built up around the athlete may not be sustained by the burden of evidential proof. Nonetheless, these

The 1936 Olympic Long Jump Medal Ceremony, left, Naoto Tajima of Japan (bronze), centre, Jesse Owens of the United States (gold), right, Luz Long of Germany (silver).

victories initially inspired a later generation of African-American athletes who would use the Olympic Games in a far more direct manner to highlight issues of racial inequality.

Performing Victory in Mexico City

The image of the victorious athlete saluting the national anthem while stood on the Olympic podium has carried great symbolic weight since it was first introduced at the Lake Placid winter Games of 1932.[27] A generation later, this performative ceremony would be exploited as a means to launch a highly controversial political protest. On the 16 October 1968, at the Mexico City Games, two African-American athletes, Tommie Smith and John Carlos, walked towards the victory podium to receive their medals, having finished first and third, respectively, in the men's 200-metre final. Both athletes were notably shoeless, wearing only black socks. Smith had draped a black scarf around his neck and Carlos, African beads, and each was wearing a single black glove, Smith on his right hand, Carlos on his left. In addition, both wore badges bearing the letters OPHR, the acronym for the Olympic Project for Human Rights. As the 'Star-Spangled Banner' began to play, Smith and Carlos slowly raised their gloved fists into the air and bowed their heads solemnly. As Smith explained in the immediate aftermath of the incident:

> My raised right hand stood for the power in black America. Carlos's raised left hand stood for the unity of black America. Together they formed an arch of unity and power. The black scarf around my neck stood for black pride. The black socks with no shoes stood for black poverty in racist America. The totality of our effort was the regaining of black dignity.[28]

The political gesture performed by Smith and Carlos soon attracted the attention of the world's media, not least because this was only the second Games to have live television images beamed around the world by satellite.[29] In the brief period it had taken to play the American national anthem, both athletes had produced a potent visual signifier of Olympic protest that transformed the perceived role of the athlete within the Olympic movement. The passive sports performer now took on the mantle of political activist, an individual willing to transgress convention and expectation to ensure that minority voices were heard in the wider public arena. And here it was the power of the visual image of that protest in the form of photographs and television pictures disseminated throughout the world that ensured the efficacy of Smith and Carlos's remarkable performative gesture.

The podium protest was in many respects the culmination of a series of actions designed to challenge racism not only in the United States, but also in South Africa and Southern Rhodesia. Prior to the Games, Smith and Carlos, along with other Mexico City Olympic medallists including Lee Evans, were students at San José State University and members of what had come to be called the 'Speed City' athletics team. San José State, however, was known at the time for far more than its athletics prowess. Under the influence of Sociologist Harry Edwards, the college was becoming a hotbed of political radicalism, gaining renown for its political activism in support of the Civil Rights movement. In 1967 Edwards launched the Olympic Project for Human Rights, an anti-racism organization that called for a boycott of the forthcoming Olympic Games by African-American athletes. In essence, the OPHR condemned what it called the double standards deployed in the United States whereby the successes of African-American athletes were celebrated

American Athletes Tommie Smith (centre) and John Carlos (right) Raising Gloved Fists on the Victor's Podium at the 1968 Mexico City Olympic Games; the Australian athlete Peter Norman is on the left.

internationally as evidence of racial harmony while segregation continued to be practiced domestically. Among the demands made by the OPHR were the reinstatement of Muhammad Ali's world title (after the boxer had been stripped of this following his refusal to serve in Vietnam), the removal of the head of the IOC, Avery Brundage (widely held to be less than sympathetic to notions of racial equality), and the removal of South African and Southern Rhodesian white-only Olympic teams. In the end, neither the boycott, nor the first two of these demands was met. Nonetheless, Smith, Carlos and Evans remained staunchly supportive of the OPHR even after the proposed boycott failed to materialize. By the time they arrived in Mexico City, talk had shifted towards the possibility of boycotting the victory ceremonies. As things turned out, the form of protest devised by Smith and Carlos was to be far more effective than any absence. For what made their protest, and its various visual manifestations, so powerful and memorable was precisely its complexity. As Douglas Hartmann has argued, this 'gesture was full of paradox and ambiguity: at once subversive and respectful, silent but resounding, seemingly empty of political content, on the one hand, yet packed with meaning and significance on the other'.[30]

Smith and Carlos paid a heavy price for their protest. Two days later they were condemned by the IOC, suspended from the US Olympic team and sent home. Despite a heroes' welcome back at San José State, Smith and Carlos were otherwise greeted with widespread condemnation in the US press. The *Chicago Tribune* for example, condemned the 'insult' to the United States, referring to Smith and Carlos as 'renegades', while *New York Times* reporter Arthur Daley described the protest as 'disgraceful, insulting and embarrassing'.[31] *Time* magazine further manipulated this tripartite critique by transforming the Olympic motto 'Faster, Higher, Stronger' (*Citius, Altius, Fortius*) into 'Angrier, Nastier, Uglier' in its account of the actions of 16 October 1968.[32] Far worse, hate mail and even death threats were sent to both Smith and Carlos. In the wake of the recent assassinations of Martin Luther King and Senator Robert Kennedy such threats could only be taken very seriously. Further, as a consequence of the protest, both athletes were effectively ostracized from American sports organizations.

Memorializing the Moment of Protest

Extolling not just the historical importance, but also the sophistication of the form of protest used by Smith and Carlos, Hartmann has written: 'Rarely is human expression as focused, elegant and eloquent as Smith and Carlos' was that day.' It was, he continues, 'an act of inspiration, passion and originality, of sheer expressive genius – truly, by these standards or any others, a work of art'.[33] Certainly the visual impact of the gesture has etched itself upon the popular imagination. Frequently replicated on T-shirts and political posters to encapsulate the historical essence of 1968 as the year of political dissent, the Smith/Carlos Civil Rights gesture, sometimes erroneously called the Black Power Salute, has now become a familiar icon within the pantheon of Olympic imagery. In 2005 this visual signifier of political protest also acquired a new manifestation when San José State students voted to erect a monument in celebration of this historical moment in the main grounds of the campus where it all began. The resulting 7-metre-high (23-feet-high) multi-media monument, designed by the Portuguese-born, San Francisco-based artist Ricardo Gouveia, officially known as Rigo 23, represents the two athletes on the Olympic podium in the

Rigo 23, *Monument to Tommie Smith and John Carlos*, 2005, mixed media, erected on the Campus of San José State University, California.

instantly recognizable posture with fists raised and heads bowed. The inclusion of details, such as the unworn sports shoes, the competition numbers on the tracksuits and even the distinction in the bend of the arm of each athlete, all serve to evoke an overall sense of historical authenticity in the work. Indeed, the artist is also reported as having specifically used 'state-of-the-art 3D scanning technology and computer-assisted virtual imaging to take actual full-body scans of the athletes' in preparation for the construction of the final monument.[34] Yet despite this overt emphasis on a historical 'veracity', artistic interpretation is also a key component within the work. For example, one of the more striking features of the work is its adoption of polychromy. Notably, both the heads of the figures, cast in bronze, and the bodies, modelled in fibreglass

mounted around a steel structure, adopt the muted brown tones conventionally associated with the mono-chrome patina of figurative monuments. The sports costumes, however, are contrastingly manufactured from colourful, reflective, hand-made ceramic tiles. The resulting mosaic-like surface here evokes non-Western craft traditions, not least the use of ceramics within Mexican culture, thus not only referencing the site of Smith and Carlos's original protest, but also highlighting the historical links between California, as site of the monument, and its indigenous Mexican roots. Here, by combining the conventions of two different cultures, the European figurative tradition and non-Western decorative arts, the monument to Smith and Carlos potentially alludes to the duality of ethnic and national status of many Americans, thus embracing the binary nature of African-American identity while simultaneously expanding the message of racial integration into a wider ethnic context.

Yet it is as much the absence of one athlete as the presence of two that contributes towards defining the significance of the monument. In Mexico City the Australian sprinter Peter Norman took the silver medal in the men's 200-metre final and thus appeared on the Olympic podium alongside Smith and Carlos. A supporter of Aboriginal rights in his native land, Norman also openly backed Smith and Carlos by wearing an OPHR badge at the medals ceremony. In the monument, however, the second-place position on the podium, originally occupied by Norman, has been left empty. This, it should be added, is far from an oversight; indeed Norman's participation in the protest was recognized and appreciated by both Smith and Carlos; the former famously said of the Australian: 'While he didn't raise a fist, he did lend a hand.'[35] Further, Norman was specifically honoured at the official ceremony for the unveiling of the monument when he was invited not only to attend, but also to participate in a public discussion as part of the day's events.[36] Rather, the empty podium position stands as an open invitation to the modern spectator to take up this position, literally to complete the work by entering into the space of protest. Thus the monument invites the viewer not only to look upon the representation of the momentous historical event, but also physically to enter into this space and embody his or her own support for the cause of racial equality. The monumental scale of Smith and Carlos, however, simultaneously reminds the participant of his or her relative insignificance positioned alongside these giants of anti-racist political protest.

Ultimately, the widespread acknowledgement, even celebration, of the significance and historical impact of Smith and Carlos's political protest at the Olympic Games of 1968 suggests that much progress has been made with regard to the issue of race in the United States since the dark days of 1968. Indeed the public display of the Smith/Carlos monument might be read as a physical manifestation of the wider shifts in the public reading of this momentous event, reflecting the extent to which the original condemnation of the athletes has now been transformed into greater acceptance, and even popular respect. At the same time, however, the invisibility of Norman and the continuing call for others to step into his shoes reinforces the fact that there is still a long way to go before the racial equality and integration that Smith and Carlos demanded in 1968 might be conceived as anywhere near achieved.

Imaging Terror

The widespread dissemination of images of Smith and Carlos mounting their protest in Mexico City in 1968 highlights the extent to which visual culture generated within the context of the Games has increasingly reached into wider political arenas. This perhaps reached its apogee at the next summer Games held in Munich in 1972. Among the countless images produced at the first Games to be held in Germany since the infamous events in Berlin in 1936, there is one widely circulated photograph that conveys a very different range of emotional responses than those usually generated by Olympic competition. The image, taken by Associated Press photographer Kurt Strumpf on 5 September that year, shows a single masked figure stood on a balcony during the siege that has subsequently come to be known as the Munich massacre. The previous night, eight armed terrorists, members of the Black September organization, entered the lightly guarded Olympic village at the Munich Games and broke into the apartment block at 31 Connolly-strasse where thirteen members of the Israeli Olympic team were housed. Following initial resistance, two members of the team escaped but two more, Yosef Romano and Moshe Weinberg, were shot and killed. The nine remaining athletes were held hostage at gun-point. As the following morning dawned, news of the terrorist attack spread across the world. Indeed it was specifically an awareness of the global news media coverage of the Games that initially prompted the Palestinian terrorists to target Munich and to launch their demands for the release of over 200 prisoners. Over the next fifteen hours, an estimated billion tele-vision viewers tuned in to watch events unfolding before the television cameras at the Olympic village as the German police attempted to negotiate with the chief terrorist, known by the pseudonym Issa. By 10:30 p.m. that night, the German authorities agreed to transfer both terrorists and hostages to Fürsten-feldbruck airport where the final dramatic moments of the siege were played out. As the German police attempted what has been widely described as a bungled rescue attempt, the hostage takers turned on their captives, killing all nine.[37] Amid mixed reports, some of which initially claimed that the rescue attempt had been a success, news finally filtered through of the tragic end to the siege. The shock of the wider international community was perhaps best captured in the voice of America's ABC television sports broad-caster Jim McKay who solemnly announced to the viewing public:

When I was a kid my father used to say 'our greatest hopes and our worst fears are seldom realized'. Our worst fears have been realised tonight. They've now said that there were eleven hostages. Two were killed in their rooms yesterday morning. Nine were killed at the airport tonight. They're all gone.[38]

The simplicity, sincerity and pathos of McKay's final sentence still stands as something of an emotional epitaph to the lost athletes, all of whom were mourned the following morning at a hastily arranged memorial service at the Olympic stadium. 80,000 spectators and 3,000 fellow athletes were in attendance as the Olympic flag was lowered to half-mast. Public anger, however, was directed not just against the terrorists. The previous morning, while the siege was under way, competition at the Games had continued and it was not until 3:15 p.m. that afternoon (over ten hours after the siege had begun) that the IOC finally decided to

Kurt Strumpf, *Black September Terrorist on the Balcony of the Israeli Team Headquarters in the Olympic Village, Munich 1972.*

suspend competition.[39] Earlier that day, Head of the IOC Avery Brundage had even resisted calls for an emergency executive board meeting.[40] When Brundage subsequently used his speech at the memorial ceremony not only to mourn the lost athletes but also to reference the 'naked political blackmail' of the African nations who had successfully campaigned for the expulsion of Rhodesia from the Games, the IOC was widely criticized and Brundage was swiftly persuaded to issue a statement of regret for this inclusion.[41] In a much quoted statement, Brundage nonetheless insisted that 'The Games must go on'. Despite the fact that the entire Israeli team, and athletes from several other nations, returned home events were recommenced that very afternoon.

It is in this context that Strumpf's image of the single terrorist stood on the balcony of 31 Connollystrasse proves so disturbing. On the one hand, this lone figure clearly signifies the dark shadow of terror cast over the Olympic Games. His spectral appearance, exaggerated by the skull-like balaclava he wears, hovers like an ill omen threatening the peaceful intentions of the international Olympic movement, while the facelessness of the figure simultaneously suggests an unthinking automaton, a machine programmed to commit atrocities without recourse to human or moral values. Further, the isolation of the figure stands as a cipher not only for the minority group he represents, but also potentially for any number of similarly minded minority groups with a political axe to grind. Much as the mass media had enabled the Games to expand into global markets, the ease with which the Games could now be hijacked for political ends potentially threatened the very existence of the Olympic movement. At the same time, however, Strumpf's image foregrounds the moral dilemma faced by the German authorities. The grainy quality of the photograph,

and its compressed depth of field, suggests a distant, surveillance shot through a telephoto lens, the terrorist seemingly unaware that he is being watched so closely. Given the context of the moment, and a post-event awareness of its outcome, it is all too easy to equate this image with a view through the telescopic sight of a police sniper. In this context, the power and authority of the terrorist is simultaneously diminished by his frailty and vulnerability to attack, exposed in an inhuman, concrete world. The power of the image thus lies in this duality of threat and vulnerability, and in putting the viewer in a morally contentious position, not least because the decision to use marksmen in a rescue attempt clearly contributed to the loss of the nine remaining Israeli hostages. Strumpf's photograph thus succeeds in articulating the full complexity of the narrative of 5 September 1972, compressing the horror of the events into one simple, but powerful, image.

Remembering the Victims

The last word, and indeed image, in this episode, however, must go to the victims of this atrocity rather than the perpetrators. Since the events of September 1972, many memorials have been erected to honour the eleven Israeli victims of the Munich massacre, some at the site of the atrocity itself, others in the athletes' own homeland.[42] One of the most striking of these is the David Berger National Memorial erected in front of the Mayfield Jewish Community Centre, in Cleveland, Ohio in 1975. The monument was commissioned by the family and friends of Berger, the Cleveland-born weightlifter and member of the Israeli Olympic team who died that night in Munich. It is dedicated to the memory of all eleven athletes. Designed by the Romanian-born, Paris-trained sculptor

David E. Davis, *The David Berger National Memorial*, 1975, bronze; in Cleveland, Ohio.

David E. Davis, the work stands at over 4 metres (13 feet) in height and is constructed from simple geometrical components consisting of ten half rings mounted on a circular base supported by eleven pillars. For this work, Davis used what at the time was regarded as a relatively new material, Cor-Ten steel, renowned for the ever-changing quality of its surface due to continuing oxidization. In scale, material and form, Davis's monument adopts the then dominant Minimalist aesthetic, as exemplified in the work of contemporary sculptors such as Richard Serra and Antony Caro. However, where these latter artists typically use monumental, geometrical forms in an abstract, non-representational way, the Berger monument was specifically designed to carry a more direct meaning. Here, the broken rings symbolize the fracturing of the Olympic spirit in Munich, while the pillars represent each of the fallen athletes. The sense of a great weight

carried also references Berger's own sport, as well as the more metaphorical burden as a consequence of the tragedy. Even the oxidization process, constantly changing the outward appearance of the monument, suggests the passage of time since the Munich Games, and the shifting memories and emotions that this inevitably brings.

As the 40th anniversary of the Munich massacre approaches, the Berger Memorial offers a timely reminder of the most notorious transgression against the peaceful objectives of international Olympic competition and of the continuing vulnerability of the Games to terrorism. Yet while Strump's terrifying image will doubtless continue to be used as a visual cipher for the events of 5 September 1972, in the end it is the victims of the atrocity who should take centre stage, to be properly remembered and commemorated.

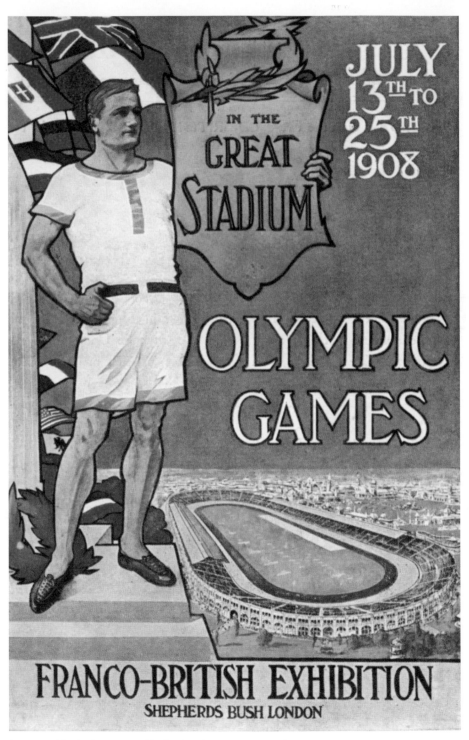

Image used for both poster and leaflet for the 1908 London Olympic Games.

seven

PROMOTING THE GAMES: PUBLICITY AND THE OFFICIAL OLYMPIC POSTER

At ancient Olympia, it was not only the athletes who travelled great distances to attend the Games. Spectators too, came from far and wide both to witness the sporting events and to participate in the public ceremonies. In the modern era, the Olympic Games would again attract large crowds of spectators, although it took a few years before the widespread popularity of the Games would be fully assured. At Athens in 1896, the festival got off to a good start as far as popular spectatorship was concerned. Here, the specially reconstructed Panathenaic stadium was frequently filled to its 60,000 capacity while, according to the Official Report, additional crowds of up to 150,000 lined the streets and hills surrounding the stadium on the day of the opening ceremony.[1] Sadly, the same could not be said for the next three Olympic festivals. In Paris (1900), St Louis (1904) and London (1908), popular interest in the sports competitions taking place under the Olympic banner was undoubtedly diminished as a consequence of the Games being subsumed into larger international exhibitions and spread out over a period of several months. Recognizing the failures of the previous two festivals to attract large spectator audiences, the organizers of the London Games made a concerted effort to address this problem by constructing a purpose-built stadium, capable of seating 68,000 and with standing room for many

more. This spectacular architectural setting, they hoped, might help to draw in the mass crowds already attending the Franco-British Exhibition. In the end, however, the tide of spectator apathy that had characterized both the Paris and St Louis Games was hardly stemmed and much of the stadium remained sparsely populated during competition. Lack of interest, however, was not deemed a major factor here. Rather, blame was apportioned to a combination of high ticket prices and poor advertising. Thus the *Daily Mail*, quoting a representative of a major ticketing agency, claimed:

> Day by day, thousands upon thousands of people are visiting the White City, but little or nothing is done to draw their attention to the fact that within a hundred yards of them athletic contests of surpassing interest are taking place. They see the wall of a structure which they may or may not identify as a Stadium, and here and there they may see notices that firework displays may be seen there on certain evenings. Why should not huge posters be displayed in such a way that visitors could not but know that at certain hours certain events were being decided?[2]

This absence of publicity had been a notable feature of all the Games to date. Indeed, in an era in which

THE SPHERE

AN ILLUSTRATED NEWSPAPER FOR THE HOME

Volume XXXIV. No. 443. London, July 18, 1908. Price Sixpence.

THE ROYAL PARTY AT THE OPENING OF THE OLYMPIC GAMES IN THE STADIUM

The Royal party (including Edward VII and Queen Alexandra) at the 1908 London Olympic games, from *The Sphere* (July 1908).

the advertising poster was at its apex in terms of both quantity and quality of production, it is striking that none of the early Olympic festivals had produced an official poster promoting the Games as a whole, although some had been produced to advertise individual events. In this context, the *Daily Mail* commentary is all the more striking for, as Margaret Timmers has shown, visual material promoting the Games had, in fact, been prominently displayed at the entrance to the Franco–British exhibition in White City. Selected by the British Olympic Committee from

competition entries, this example might thus be considered the first official publicity poster for the Games. It certainly heralded a practice that has continued unabated to this day. Indeed Olympic posters have subsequently become one of the most powerful visual expressions associated with the Olympic movement. Their development, the increasing diversity of their forms and the complex meanings they have sought to convey provide an intriguing visual history of the Games.

Waving the Flag

Though modest in appearance, the London poster of 1908 established some basic design principles that would variously be adopted, adapted and rejected over the course of the next century. The image is dominated by the representation of a monumental athlete in sports costume. The professional running shoes suggest athletics, although the pose, hand on hip and holding an olive crowned shield, is notably passive. This lends the athlete a decidedly sculptural appearance, not least because he stands on what appears to be a plinth – the victory podium would not be introduced to the Games for another 24 years. The figure towers over a topographical representation of the location of the Games, with the Great Stadium in White City prominent in the foreground. Behind the athlete, the flags of many nations form a colourful backdrop. Perhaps unsurprisingly, the Union Jack takes pride of place at the apex, thus reflecting Edwardian Britain's confident sense of its own place in the world. The explicit inclusion of national flags in this first Olympic poster carried much significance for the moment of production. Although Coubertin had initially intended that the Olympic Games would be 'competitions between athletes in individual or team events and not between countries' – a concept still enshrined in article 6 of the Olympic charter – nationalist interests had early impacted upon the Games.[3] Notably this was to come to a particular head in London when several incidents marred the relationship between the teams of Britain and the United States. The most famous of these incidents involved Ralph Rose, flag bearer for the US team at the opening ceremony. Even before the ceremony had begun it was noted that the national flags of all participating nations except Sweden and the United States were on display at the stadium. Lord Desborough, President of the Organizing Committee would later offer an apology for this oversight.[4] Then, during the procession Rose, supported by many of his Irish-American teammates, refused to dip the Stars and Stripes as he passed before King Edward VII, reportedly a gesture of solidarity to supporters of Irish independence.[5] Notably, a number of Irish athletes had sought to appear at the Games representing their own nation, but had been instructed that they could only participate as members of the British team. In protest, some withdrew while others deliberately separated themselves from the British contingent when marching in the opening ceremony.[6]

It was an incident in the final of the 400-metre race, however, that most highlighted the fragility of international relations between the British and American teams. In the home straight, American sprinter John C. Carpenter narrowly led his British opponent Wyndham Halswelle. Shortly after he crossed the line, however, it was announced by the all-British team of judges that Carpenter had been disqualified for elbowing his opponent. The US team was incensed by what it regarded as high-handed and unfair treatment and immediately lodged an official protest. But this was to no avail. The race was declared null and void and scheduled to be re-run a few days later. As the other competitors were all compatriots of Carpenter, the US team boycotted the race in protest, thus leaving Halswelle in the embarrassing position of having to run alone to secure his medal.[7] Throughout the Games further accusations of bias were directed towards the British judges by the US team, so that by the end of the Games, there was notable bad feeling between the two nations. As one contemporary popular journal reported:

> The idea that international assemblies of any kind do the State good in promoting peace is one which is rapidly being blown into splinters. More bad blood was caused between otherwise friendly nations by the late Olympic Games than by all the diplomatic incidents in the last ten years together.[8]

The literal flag waving that had characterized the opening ceremony in London was thus now taking on a more sinister metaphorical connotation.

While not consequent to the events that transpired in White City, it is at least noteworthy here that the official poster for the London Games not only privileged the Union Jack, but also confined 'Old Glory' to a miniscule representation in the background of the image. Perhaps, indeed, this poster offers some visual evidence that Britain had not been as fully respectful of its transatlantic neighbour and major sporting competitor prior to, as well as during, the Games as it might have been.

Despite the problems generated by rampant nationalism at the London Games, flag waving would also feature prominently in the poster for the Games of 1912 in Stockholm. Designed by the Swedish Royal Academician, Olle Hjortzberg, the Stockholm image represents a group of naked male youths performing

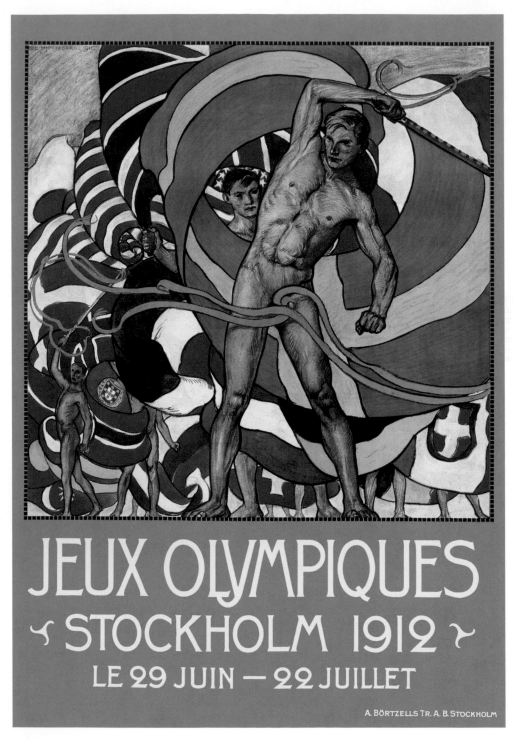

Olle Hjorztberg, poster for the 1912 Stockholm Olympic Games.

a 'march of nations' while waving the national symbols of 22 of the 28 nations participating at the Games. Again, the prominence of the flag of the home nation is hardly surprising, though the strong focus on Britain and the United States at the relative expense of France, founding nation of the modern Olympic Games, certainly raised a few eyebrows. Though not elaborating on the point, the Official Report of the Stockholm Games did acknowledge that criticism had been received from 'diplomatic quarters' concerning the 'order in which the various standards were shown on the poster' and that this had led, in some instances to 'a disinclination . . . to exhibit it'.[9] In a somewhat disingenuous riposte to such accusations, the Report claimed that the ordering of the flags 'was determined by coloristic, and not political, reasons'.[10]

In visual terms, Hjortzberg's emphasis upon flags explicitly links the Stockholm poster to its precedent at the London Games of 1908. In terms of production and distribution, however, the Swedish Olympic Committee was operating on an entirely different scale. For the Stockholm Games nearly 90,000 posters were produced in sixteen different languages while the same corporate image was also used in leaflets and on stamps.[11] These posters were subsequently distributed for display at railway stations and hotels throughout Europe and the United States, and even as far afield as Australia, China, Japan and South Africa. Not content with this alone, the organizers even issued the following call to its fellow citizens:

> We take the liberty of calling your attention to the extraordinary importance of an effective and systematically organized advertisement abroad of the approaching Olympic Games, and hereby appeal to Swedish business men travelling abroad, to support us in this matter by carrying with them

on their journeys and – eventually, in co-operation with the various Swedish Consulates which have undertaken the chief distribution for their respective cities – to distribute in some suitable way, not only the programme and the little descriptive pamphlet of the Games, which are published in English, French, German and Swedish, but also the *advertising stamp* and, most especially, the large *poster of the Games*.[12]

The professionalism of the Swedish promotional campaign probably did much to put the Olympic Games on the international map as well as enticing new spectator audiences. From this point on, the official Olympic poster would play a vital role in the wider Olympic publicity drive and become an established element within the Games.

Classical Resonances

The sculptural qualities of the figures represented in both the London and Stockholm posters echo the continuing resonances of the classical heritage on the Games themselves. In particular, the explicit nudity of Hjortzberg's flag wavers, though raising questions of moral propriety in some nations, makes a clear allusion to antique figurative monuments.[13] In the inter-war years, these overt references to antiquity would continue to make notable appearance in Olympic posters.

When the national competitiveness that had expressed itself so forcefully at the London Games exploded into major military conflict in 1914, the future of the Olympic movement looked bleak. Nonetheless the IOC continued to discuss plans for future Olympic festivals during the early months of the conflict, presumably like so many hoping that it

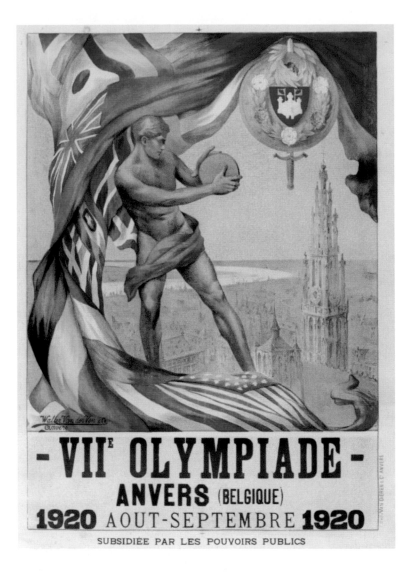

Walter van der Ven and Martha van Kuyck, poster for the 1920 Antwerp Olympic Games.

would all be over by Christmas. Stalemate on the Western front, however, soon put paid to all hopes of staging the Olympics in 1916. Following the Armistice, the IOC swiftly adopted plans to stage the Games of the seventh Olympiad in 1920. In a spirit of solidarity with the nation whose invasion by German forces had been the catalyst for much of the fighting, the IOC awarded the Games to Belgium, with the city of Antwerp playing host to the first post-war Olympics.

With little over a year to prepare, and at a time of deep financial crisis, not everyone felt that this was a blessing.[14] Despite the organizational pressures, however, an official Olympic poster was early designed, printed and distributed throughout the world. Adopting a similar format to the London poster, this work featured a monumental discus thrower towering above the cityscape of Antwerp, festooned with swirls of cloth representing the national flags of the competing nations.

Listed in the Official Report as the work of Walter van der Ven, it represents a discus thrower clearly based on a monument produced a century earlier by the neo-classical sculptor Matthias Kessels.[15] A bronze copy of the marble original had also been cast and put on display in the Gardens of the Palais des Academies in Brussels as recently as 1880. The decision to include a representation of Kessels' sculpture in the Antwerp poster is an intriguing one. As a Maastricht-born sculptor, Kessels is conventionally identified as a Dutch artist, though at the time he produced his *Discus Thrower* much of modern-day Belgium remained part of the broader United Kingdom of the Netherlands. Thus from a Belgian perspective in 1920, Kessels could be identified either as a neighbouring invader or a son of the soil. Enveloped by the swirling flags of the community of nations (which also add a touch of strategic modesty) and in the pro-internationalist context of the Olympic movement, Kessels's *Discus Thrower* signifies a link both to the past and to the present. On the one hand, in a post-war context the inclusion of a classical discobolus, albeit one redefined in early nineteenth-century neoclassical form, clearly referenced the ancient Olympics. At the same time this inevitably drew attention to the military truce practiced in ancient Greece during the period of the Games, something that, as contemporaries knew only too well, had not occurred during the recent conflict. On the other hand, the intertwining of flags around an image of sport situated geographically in the city of Antwerp, proposed a more conciliatory present where nation states could compete on the playing fields rather than the battlefields of Flanders. As if to reinforce this rejection of military conflict the shield and sword that form the coat of arms of Antwerp are here garlanded with flowers, the circular form of the shield echoing that of the discus held in the hand of the frozen athlete. This re-focus on peace and international cooperation was also reflected in other activities introduced for the first time at Antwerp. Thus the release of doves of peace and the official declaration of the Olympic Oath were both introduced at the Games of 1920. Furthermore, the Olympic flag, designed by Coubertin in 1914, was also flown for the first time, its five interlocking rings symbolizing the union of the five continents. The poster for the Antwerp Games had thus explicitly deployed Classicism to signify peace and internationalism. Sixteen years later National Socialist Germany would exploit a similar vocabulary, but to very different ends.

By the 1930s publicizing the Games had become a major factor within the staging of Olympic festivals.

Hitler greeting the Olympic flame, Berlin, 1936.

Franz Würbel, poster for the 1936 Berlin Olympic Games.

Poster for the 1924 Winter Olympic Games.

Recognizing the political value of staging the Games as a showcase for the new National Socialist regime, the German Organizing Committee certainly put their full force behind this process, handing over responsibility for all publicity to the Ministry for Propaganda. As early as 1934, an official poster competition had been launched and 59 submissions received. Although several prizes were awarded, all these designs were rejected as 'unsatisfactory', an indication of the importance afforded by the regime to the official image of the Games.[16] The following year a smaller group of artists was reconvened and commissioned to produce new designs. From these, Franz Würbel's powerful image of an olive-wreath-clad Olympic victor emerging from behind the looming presence of the Brandenburg Gate was now accepted as the official poster for the Games. Würbel's image conforms both to the ideological and the artistic conventions of the National Socialist regime. Here an instantly recognizable national symbol – Berlin's famous neoclassical monument first erected in the late eighteenth century – is aligned with a colossal, classically inspired and imposing figure rising up, phoenix-like, in the background. The officially sanctioned notion that National Socialist Germany was the sole and natural heir to the antique world is thus given explicit visual form. The low viewpoint and commanding presence of both these symbols further exudes a sense of power and authority. Even the Olympic rings, by now such a resonant symbol of internationalism, are here represented as uniquely adorning the head of this monumental personification of German might, who seemingly challenges all-comers to dispute his ownership of the classical heritage. The Official Report described this figure as raising his right arm 'in the Olympic greeting'.[17] Certainly the straight arm salute first adopted by the French team at the Antwerp Games

in 1920 had been accepted as an official Olympic salute by the time of the Paris Games of 1924, as evidenced by the official poster produced by Jean Droit. The appropriation of this gesture by the National Socialist Party, however, ensured that while Würbel's poster could justifiably claim to be articulating support for the Olympic movement, there would be little doubt in the minds of many spectators that this salute was simultaneously honouring Adolf Hitler, *Führer* of the Third Reich. Like other famous manifestations of National Socialist culture at the Berlin Games, including Leni Riefenstahl's *Olympia* and Werner March's Olympiastadion, Würbel's Olympic poster has come to signify a dark chapter in Olympic history, even as the simplicity and effectiveness of the graphic design might be grudgingly admired.

Does Classicism Have a Future?

There can be little doubt that the appropriation of Classicism by National Socialist Germany generated something of a conundrum for future Olympic poster designers. In the immediate wake of the Second World War, for example, the celebration of an authoritarian classicist mode of representation could all too easily be linked with the tragic endgame of the holocaust. In the first post-war Games, however, the direct association between ancient Greece and the modern Olympic Games was once again foregrounded, though perhaps with a subtle critique of the Nazi appropriation of the past. The Games of 1948, held in war-weary London, epitomized the mend-and-make-do attitude of austerity Britain. Shortages in both housing and food were a constantly referenced feature of the Games and even the official poster, designed by Walter Herz, was produced to a tight budget and timetable.[18] This first post-Second World War Olympic poster notably

Walter Herz,
poster for the
1948 London
Olympic Games.

adopted a similar configuration to the Antwerp poster of 28 years earlier. Here a sculptural monument of a discus thrower is superimposed upon an image of a tower, again an architectural icon geographically signifying the location of the Games. The furled and intertwined international flags of the earlier image, however, have here been replaced with the simplicity of the Olympic rings, similarly highlighting the importance of international cooperation. Yet in contrast to the Berlin poster, the rings are now brought into the lower foreground as if offered to, rather than kept from, the spectator. The representation of the clock tower of the Houses of Parliament as the principal

geographical signifier within the image, also suggests a contrast with the Berlin poster. Here, rather than invading the spectator's space the architectural feature stands tall, but modestly, in the background, a symbolic memorial to the endurance and stoicism of Britain and its resistance to war-time invasion. It was the inclusion of Myron's *Discobolus*, however, that most directly challenged the ideological claims of a now defeated National Socialist Germany.

Reifenstahl's famous inclusion of Myron's iconic work in the opening sequences of *Olympia*, and its visual metamorphosis into a contemporary German athlete, was certainly one of the most explicit appropriations

Hitler with Myron's *Discobolus*, 1938.

of the classical legacy of the Games visually enacted by the National Socialist state. Indeed the mapping of this ideological claim onto a familiar visual signifier was further reinforced in 1938 when German authorities secured the purchase of the first, and most famous, version of the *Discobolus*, unearthed at the Villa Palombara near Rome in 1781. The transference of the Palombara *Discobolus* from the Italian capital to the Glyptothek Museum in Munich was something of a propaganda coup. Certainly Hitler was keen to be photographed alongside this important acquisition. However, a second version of the *Discobolus* had also been discovered in 1790 and acquired for the British collector Charles Townley. By 1805 this work had entered the British Museum in London, where it has resided ever since. The Townley *Discobolus* is easily distinguished from the Palombara version as a consequence of an erroneous restoration. Whereas evidence from classical sources clearly suggests that the head should be raised and looking back towards the discus, as in the Palombara version, the Townley *Discobolus* looks down towards the ground. Hence it is clearly this version, as opposed to the one purchased by Hitler, that occupies centre-stage in the London poster.[19] By placing the *Discobolus* at the very centre of his composition, Herz thus reclaimed both Myron's work and the wider classical heritage from its earlier appropriation by National Socialism. Further, by realigning this powerful visual signifier with the Olympic movement, the *Discobolus* effectively reacquired a universal identity. The fact that it was this very same year that the Palombara *Discobolus* returned to Rome as part of a post-war reparation programme, adds a further topicality and significance to the dominant presence of the *Discobolus* in the London Olympic poster. It might also be added that Herz's explicit articulation of the lines of fracture in the neck, shoulder and arm

of Myron's work foreground the very imperfections so anomalous to National Socialist ideology, while the bowed head adds a further sense of solemnity at a time when the memory of those who had suffered during the conflict was still fresh in the minds of all those attending the Games.

Breaking Tradition: The Sixties Revolution and Beyond

The staging of the Olympic Games in Tokyo in 1964 and Mexico City in 1968 respectively was a strong indication of a shift in emphasis within the Olympic movement. Prior to this, every previous summer and winter Games, with the exception of Melbourne in 1956, had been held in either Europe or the United States. Bringing the Games to new venues in Asia and Latin America not only enhanced the international credentials of the Games and reached out to new audiences. It also reflected changing attitudes in global politics in a post-colonial era. In promoting these Games, however, the replication of the same visual vocabularies widely used in earlier Olympic festivals clearly risked undermining the very expansionism and cultural openness that the IOC sought in selecting these venues in the first place. Accordingly, overt references to the classical origins of the Games in the imagery used in Olympic posters during this period virtually disappeared. More modernist-inspired designs now began to emerge, as epitomized in Yusaku Kamekura's 'Rising Sun' poster for the Tokyo Games of 1964. Clearly inspired by the 'less is more' ideology of the Minimalist movement in contemporary Western art, Kamekura here reduced Olympic symbolism to its barest essentials, a red circle hovering over gold Olympic rings on a white background. Notably, Kamekura's design operated as far more than

Yusaku Kamekura, poster for the 1964 Tokyo Olympic Games.

Lance Wyman, poster for the 1968 Mexico City Olympic Games.

simply a poster, effectively becoming the corporate logo for the Games and appearing on a wide range of products from lapel pins to luggage labels. Three other posters were also produced, each, however, also carrying the Rising Sun emblem.[20] By now posters were rapidly becoming just one component in a wider, highly sophisticated and professionalized graphic programme designed to confer a visual identity on the Games. Kamekura's design, in its graphic simplicity, clearly evokes the Japanese national flag. Like Ichikawa's cinematic focus on a more literal rising sun in the opening sequence to *Tokyo Olympiad*, this went some considerable way towards rehabilitating the image of the Japanese flag in the broader international community. Here, the prior associations of this powerful symbol with the Imperialism of the 1930s and '40s gave way to a more open affiliation with the peaceful ideology of Olympism. Indeed, this widely disseminated visual signifier was an integral element within the broader objectives of staging the Games in Tokyo; namely to signal the re-emergence of post-war Japan on the world stage.

Where the Tokyo poster referenced Minimalism in its design, the Mexico City Games of 1968 exploited the then highly fashionable visual vocabulary of Op Art. Once again, the poster design was a key element within a much wider programme conferring a strong and readily recognizable corporate image to the Games. In this poster, a geometrical latticework of straight lines and curves radiates out from a central typographical representation of the words 'Mexico 68', creating a pulsating visual illusion of constant vibration and motion. While overtly referencing the contemporaneity of modernist-inspired Op Art, however, the Mexico 68 design simultaneously alludes to the indigenous abstract forms of Mexican folk culture. Thus the image conflates both national and international

cultural references and reinforces links between tradition and modernity.

Poster Explosion

By the 1970s, the publicity machine of the Olympic Games had moved on a long way from the one-off poster designs of the early twentieth century. The publicity programmes for each Olympic Games now expanded considerably, becoming increasingly sophisticated and collective enterprises orchestrated and executed by large teams of graphic designers. The single official poster thus gave way to a series of posters incorporating emblems, mascots and pictograms, all combining to articulate an officially sanctioned, though broadly defined, image of the Games as orchestrated by the National Olympic Committees.

At the Munich Games of 1972, for example, poster production reached virtually an industrial scale. A Department of Visual Design, headed by Otl Aicher, was established several years in advance of the Games and advertising posters were already being distributed fully two years before the Olympics commenced. Individual posters were produced for each of the 21 sports, as well as a generic poster, each adopting the same colour scheme and typography. Furthermore, several more designs advertised the breadth of cultural activities that accompanied the Games while the Organizing Committee even established competitions for individual designs for African and Latin American nations.[21] One of the most striking departures from previous Olympic poster production, however, was the plan to commission a number of contemporary artists to produce a series of posters which would then be put on sale in limited editions to help finance the Games. The first of the so-called 'Edition Olympia' series appeared in October 1969, and featured seven poster

Poster for the 2008 Beijing Olympic Games.

designs. By the time of the Games, four more series, each with seven poster designs, had been published. Among the best known artists commissioned for this project were Josef Albers, Eduardo Chillida, Hans Hartung, David Hockney, Allen Jones, R. B. Kitaj, Oskar Kokoschka, Jacob Lawrence, Pierre Soulages and Tom Wesselmann.[22] The commission for the series stipulated that artists need 'not be limited by a connection to the Olympics in the contents of his work', but that it was 'desirable that there would be a thematic relation to sports or the Olympiad in Munich'. Relatively few of the artists included in the final series of art posters paid much heed to the latter request, the notable exceptions being Hockney's diver, Kitaj's swimmer and Lawrence's black athletes striving for the finishing line. The art posters produced for the Munich Games notably re-invoked the importance of the official connection between art and the Olympic Games that Coubertin had earlier, if unsuccessfully, striven to promote. The fact that so many of the artists involved continued to ignore the sport theme perhaps goes some way towards explaining why the official Olympic art competitions, first staged in 1912, but abandoned by 1948, ultimately failed.[23]

Towards the Global Games

By the end of the twentieth century and the beginning of the twenty-first, as the Games themselves were increasingly staged in new geographical locations, visual references to local, indigenous cultures would also increasingly permeate Olympic posters and publicity imagery. Thus at the Seoul Games of 1988, a variation of a popular Korean decorative symbol was adopted as an emblem and used on posters to promote the Games. As the Official Report pointed out:

The emblem embraced the five Olympic rings on top of the *samtaeguk,* a traditional Korean pattern and visual image representing Korea. The pattern is well known among Koreans, being widely used as decoration on fans, the gates of Korean-style homes, artifacts and folk crafts.[24]

More recently, the running figure on a red background in the poster for the Beijing Games of 2008 was based on a modified version of the Chinese calligraphic character 'jing', part of the two characters that articulate the name of the Chinese capital city.[25] Similarly, the emblem used for the Vancouver winter Olympic Games of 2010 was based on an *inukshuk*, or stone figure, found in the Arctic region of Canada and associated with Inuit culture.[26] This diversity of design within Olympic posters produced in recent decades provides visual evidence of a significant move away from the popular use of the archetypal white, male, physically idealized athlete as a cipher for Olympic sport. The presence and successes of both female and non-European athletes at the Games have inevitably highlighted the limitations of this image while the increasing media coverage of the Paralympic Games has contributed further towards recognition that visual representations of the sporting body should indeed adopt a significantly wider range of forms if they are in any way to reflect the realities of contemporary practices. To this day, official Olympic posters retain their status as the most familiar visual expression of the Games. The demand to encapsulate the broad meaning and significance of individual, geographically and temporally located Olympic festivals continues to offer a challenge to artists and graphic designers as visual culture continues to play a vital role in defining the mass experience of the sporting festival that is the Olympic Games.

eight

DESIGNS ON THE OLYMPICS: FROM STADIA TO SPORTING PARAPHERNALIA

The staging of Olympic festivals at different international venues every four years has undoubtedly served to expand global interest in, and enhance the reputation of, the Games. At the same time, this peripatetic existence has enabled the constant renewal and reinvention of key infrastructural elements of the Games as each National Olympic Committee has striven to forge its own unique identity. In this context, the work of a whole host of often anonymous individuals, from architects and engineers to planners and graphic designers, has helped to shape the overall vision of the Games as delivered at each unique Olympic festival. The specific design of Olympic stadia, frequently the visual centrepiece of each Games, provides just one example of this. While the basic function of the stadium has remained essentially the same, namely to facilitate the practice of a range of sporting activities and enable spectators to view these activities in reasonable comfort, the stylistic and symbolic forms adopted in the architecture for each stadium have been widely divergent. This, in turn, has invoked different notions of what characterizes the relationship between each site and the Games as a broader concept. For example, the overt classical affiliations of the ancient Panathenaic stadium in Athens, carefully restored in time for the inaugural Games of 1896, ensured that the historical link between the original and modern Games was foremost in the minds of those both participating in, and attending, the Games. By 1908, however, a more functional approach to stadium design was taking precedent, as evidenced by the building of the Great Stadium at White City in London. Here, the open ended, horseshoe structure of the Panathenaic stadium, with its sharp bends, a typical characteristic of ancient sporting arenas, gave way to a more rationally laid out track, enabling athletes to corner at speed. While the Great Stadium was not the first athletics facility designed in this format, it did constitute the first purpose-built Olympic stadium for large spectator audiences adopting this configuration. The fact that this format also enabled other popular spectator activities, such as football matches, to be staged in the centre-field was doubtless also a major consideration.

From a more aesthetic point of view, the architect Jan Wils designed one of the most striking of the early Olympic stadia, for the Amsterdam Games of 1928. A founder member of the De Stijl art group and a major player in the Amsterdam School of modernist architects and designers, Wils's geometrically simple, red brick stadium consciously adopted a style more reminiscent of contemporary factories and warehouses, thus embracing the utopian architectural vocabulary that was already sweeping through much of Europe in the post-First World War era.[1] Its low-slung profile,

Jan Wils, stadium designed for the 1928 Amsterdam Olympic Games.

punctuated by a tall tower, also notably invoked the form of a ship, a suitably symbolic reference to Amsterdam's international maritime history and contemporary commerce. Despite Wils's introduction of a modernist vocabulary into Olympic stadia, however, Classicism would return with a vengeance in 1936 with Werner March's Berlin Olympiastadion. This declamatory building, decorated with tall columns and statues of powerful male nude figures reminiscent of ancient statues of Olympic athletes, reinforced the broadly, if controversially, defined notion that National Socialist Germany was now the natural heir to the antique world.

By the second half of the twentieth century, however, such overt paeans to Classicism were increasingly rejected and replaced by fairly conventional, functionally inspired stadium designs throughout the 1950s and '60s. During this period, however, practical necessity – the fact that many of these stadia were adapted from already existing structures – diminished the opportunity

for architects to make bold, individual statements. Indeed it was not until 1972 that an Olympic stadium design would again command the attention of the global architectural fraternity. The organizers of the Munich Games were understandably determined to resist any possible association with March's earlier Berlin stadium, and thus with Germany's National Socialist past. Accordingly, the stadium structure was carefully conceived to blend into the landscape and resist any sense of monumentality. Without doubt the most innovative and visually striking feature of the design was the tent roof, designed by Behnisch Architekten.[2] Here the use of a reinforced acrylic glass structure suspended by steel cables maintained a light and airy atmosphere within the stadium while simultaneously protecting spectators from the elements. In a radical break from previous stadium design principles, however, the roof was not restricted to the contours of the stadium itself but extended to link other sports venues and areas in the broader Olympic Park. The stadium thus appeared less as an entity in its own right and more as a kind of architectural folly situated in a carefully landscaped, green space. Its context was thus more reminiscent of an eighteenth-century English garden than a modern, urban sports arena.

Of all the Olympic stadia built to date, however, perhaps none has attracted as much critical attention as the National Stadium in Beijing, colloquially referred to as the 'Bird's Nest'. Designed by the Swiss architectural firm Herzog & de Meuron, and with artistic input from the Chinese contemporary artist Ai Weiwei, the Bird's Nest is an Olympic stadium like no other.[3] Ironically, the trademark interlacing steel beams that define the outward appearance of the building were initially designed as a means to disguise the support structure for a proposed retractable roof. Although plans to incorporate this were abandoned following the collapse of a similarly designed roof at Charles de Gaulle airport in Paris in 2004, the outer shell was retained. Herzog & de Meuron's initial inspiration for this outer form came from a study of local Chinese ceramics. The elliptical asymmetry and bulging form of the building, however, has also been interpreted as a complex and ambiguous symbol, articulating far more than simply a regional cultural reference. Thus in a *New York Times* review, architectural critic Nicolai Ouroussoff praised the 'intoxicating beauty' and 'allure' of the building, while simultaneously recognizing that the interlaced beams could be read

The Munich Olympic Stadium in the Olympiapark, Munich 1972 (photographed in 1996).

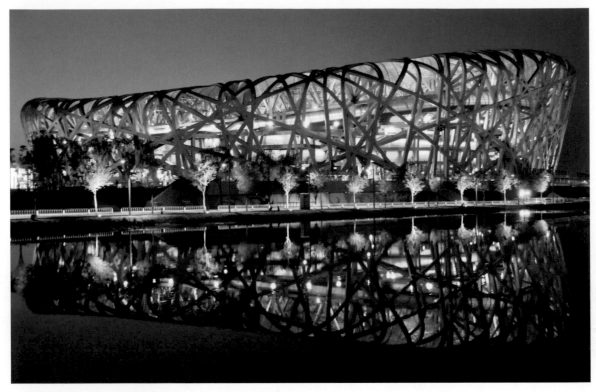

The National Stadium, Beijing (colloquially called 'The Bird's Nest'), 2008.

as 'straining to contain the forces that are pushing and pulling it this way and that'.[4] Thus, Ouroussoff continues, the architectural design foregrounds 'the tension just beneath the surface of a society in constant turmoil'.[5] The success of the Bird's Nest stadium may well lie not only in its capacity to fulfil its function both as a practical sports stadium and symbolic backdrop signifying the wider claims of national re-emergence embedded in China's staging of the Olympic Games in 2008. Simultaneously, the design encapsulates, in visual form, the wider tensions and uncertainties generated by this shift in global power relations, as witnessed both from within and without, a significant achievement that makes the Bird's Nest an iconic signifier of early twenty-first-century socio-political, as well as sporting, history.

Olympic Commodities: The Official Mascot

While the stadium has always remained the principal focus of Olympic festivals, a host of other design arte-facts have also been generated in conjunction with the Games. For example, during the latter part of the twentieth century, the global reach and mass-marketing potential of the Olympics resulted in the expansion in production of a range of souvenirs, some official others unofficial, including items as diverse as ashtrays, board games and tea cosies. One of the most popular of these mass-produced commodities has been the official Olympic mascot. Although a relatively new development as a marketing tool, the mascot may be construed to have its roots in an earlier era, dating back to the Los Angeles Games of 1932. Reportedly, on 2 January of that year, the same day that work commenced on what was to become the first official Olympic village, a small, black Scottish Terrier was born. Named Smoky, he would soon become a popular media celebrity and the first widely recognized mascot of the Olympic Games. Throughout the duration of the Los Angeles Games, Smoky lived at the Olympic Village where he was frequently seen and photographed with a host of athletes from forty different nations. He was popularly reported as 'the friend of every athlete in the Olympic Village' and the 'only inhabitant who spoke every language'.[6] Easily identified by his white coat bearing the Olympic rings and declaring his official status as 'mascot', Smoky was used by the popular press as a form of visual shorthand to signify international friendship. 'He was just a little black dog, but he did more to spread goodwill among all the athletes at the Village than any platform speaker', opined Bill Henry, Sports Editor for the *LA Times* in what virtually constituted an official obituary

for Smoky following the dog's untimely death at the hands of a hit-and-run driver in 1934.[7] The origins of Smoky's status as mascot for the Games of 1932, it must be admitted, are somewhat obscure and it seems likely that his adoption was an improvised affair, gradually hyped up by the local media. Yet, while no overt claim to official status was made on the little dog's behalf in the four-volume Official Report of the Games, a photograph of Smoky wearing his Olympic mascot coat does make a notable appearance.[8] Certainly the adoption of animal mascots for sports teams had an established history in the United States prior to 1932. For example, the Yale University athletics team is reported as keeping a bulldog mascot (named Handsome Dan) as early as 1889.[9] On this occasion, however, it was an event, rather than a team, that defined Smoky's status as mascot, and accordingly his reign as media celebrity turned out to be relatively short-lived.

'Smoky', mascot for the 1932 Los Angeles Olympic Games.

It would be another 40 years before another mascot would be officially adopted for the Olympic Games, although this time it would be a purely symbolic, rather than a living, animal. Waldi the rainbow-coloured dachshund was developed as part of the mass expansion of corporate marketing that accompanied the Munich Olympics in 1972. Unlike Smoky, however, this image was carefully manufactured from the outset and designed with two specific goals; first, to promote the Games among a younger generation and second to generate economic income for the organizers. Accordingly, versions of Waldi were produced to precise scale and colour configurations marketed under licence for reproduction either as soft toys or on badges, posters and key rings. The impact of the Waldi franchise may be measured by the reported sale of two million Waldis in over 20 countries.[10] This success, economic as well as symbolic, thus ensured that official mascots would feature prominently in the promotional material at every summer and winter Olympic Games since. Many of these designs have been fairly bland, and have failed to capture the public imagination. Two mascots, however, perhaps stand out as worthy of brief discussion.

Certainly one of the most popular and endearing was Misha the bear, official mascot of the Moscow Olympics in 1980. In advance of the Games, the Moscow Olympic Organizing Committee openly sought the support of the Soviet public, and children in particular, by inviting viewers of the popular television programme, *Animal World*, to suggest which animal they thought best represented the Russian nation (and by extension, the Soviet Union as a whole).[11] The overwhelming response called for the adoption of a bear, a widely loved character frequently appearing in Russian folk culture from fairy tales and poems to popular songs. Following up on this popular

'Misha', mascot for the 1980 Moscow Olympic Games.

approval, a second campaign was launched to select the official design for the bear, with opinions again sought from the viewers of *Animal World* as well as readers of the specialist sports newspaper *Sovetskii Sport*. The winner was Viktor Chizhikov, a well-known illustrator and caricaturist who had previously worked on a host of Soviet publications including the satirical journal *Krokodil*. Chizhikov had also, by this time, established a firm reputation as an illustrator of children's books. The final design for Misha, a fuzzy, pot-bellied bear with a wide smile,

'Cobi', mascot for the 1992 Barcelona Olympic Games.

was chosen from more than 100 versions produced by the artist. The image of Misha clearly drew on the tradition of the teddy bear, a cultural icon more typically associated with Germany and, through its original reference to President Theodore 'Teddy' Roosevelt, the United States. In this way Russian folk traditions were aligned with wider internationalist associations to signify the conventional Olympic notion of global friendship and peace. In some respects, however, this plan backfired when neither the United States, nor West Germany, participated in the widely boycotted Moscow Games. Thus the

reference ultimately lost much of its significance. Here, however, it is tempting to speculate that the animated tear shed from the eye of a colossal Misha at the closing ceremony in Moscow may have signified more than just regret at the passing of the Games themselves.[12]

Where Misha was one of the most endearing Olympic mascots, Cobi, the official mascot of the Barcelona Games of 1992, was certainly one of the more controversial. Following the established tradition of anthropomorphizing local fauna, artist Javier Mariscal based his mascot design on a Catalan sheepdog. It may be fair to say, however, that this was far from immediately evident to most spectators. Mariscal consciously rejected the cuteness that had typified previous mascots, opting instead for a more modern, edgy characterization. Visually, the most striking feature of Cobi was the explicit adoption of a Cubist vocabulary inspired by Pablo Picasso, a celebrated son of the Catalan soil. Hence, as critics were only too eager to point out, Cobi's nose somewhat eccentrically appeared in profile on the side of his face, while his eyes stared straight out. The three strands of hair that adorned Cobi's forehead also served to undermine his dog-like and cutesy qualities, implying more the comb-over of a balding, middle-aged male. Cobi was not only promoted through official merchandise, but also featured in a series of 26 half-hour television cartoons entitled *The Cobi Troupe*. Here, as the Official Report made explicit, the objective was 'not to publicize the sports but to popularize the mascot', Cobi thus signifying to the world the youthful, slightly rebellious and artistic

Medal design introduced at the 2004 Athens Olympic Games.

image of Barcelona.[13] The Olympic mascot had thus now taken on an existence of its own, beyond its affinity with the Olympic movement.

Medals and Trophies

The Olympic medal has also provided opportunity for designers to stamp their mark on the visual legacy of the Olympic Games, though here, diversity has been notably less evident. The distribution of Olympic medals, both to victors and runners-up, is very much an invention of the modern era. While victory was certainly celebrated at the ancient Games, official rewards were limited to olive wreaths and there was no recognition that finishing in second or third place was even worthy of mention, never mind reward. The first Olympic medals were accordingly awarded at Athens in 1896, though these were restricted to silver (not gold) medals for victors and bronze for second place. At the Paris Games in 1900 no medals were awarded, although a set of medals was later issued in commemoration of these Games. Thus it was not until the third Olympiad at St Louis in 1904 that the current pattern of gold for first place, silver for second and bronze for third was established. Up until this point, the medal design for each Games was unique, though all notably placed a strong emphasis upon Classicism. In 1907, however, the IOC launched a competition to develop a standardized design for the obverse of all future medals, permitting individual designs only for the reverse side. The successful design, by the Australian sculptor Bertram Mackennal, featured a nude male athlete being crowned by two young women in classical garb (thus fulfilling Coubertin's assumed ideal role for women at the Games) and was introduced for the London Games of 1908.[14] While Mackennal's design was again used in 1912, the first two Games of the interwar period (Antwerp in 1920 and Paris in 1924) inexplicably abandoned the previously established principle and produced their own designs. Once again, the classically inspired male nude athlete was made use of to symbolize Olympic victory, despite the increasing participation of women at the Olympic Games at this time. In 1928 the IOC returned to the principle of a standardized medal, and introduced a new design by the Italian artist Giuseppe Cassioli. This featured Nike, goddess of victory, carrying palm fronds and raising a victor's olive wreath above her head. On the reverse, a crowd of athletes bears aloft a victor, the scene once more overtly set at the ancient Games. Cassioli's design successfully stood the test of time. Both sides of the medal design were retained up until 1972, while the obverse was still deployed in barely modified form as late as 2000. However, to celebrate the return of the Games to Athens, a new variation was introduced in 2004, with Nike now represented hovering above the Panathenaic stadium, home to both ancient Athenian sport and the first Olympic Games of the modern epoch. It is, at the very least, striking that overt references to the classical origins of the Olympics have been retained in medal designs despite the increasingly erosion of this reference in other forms of visual culture associated with the Games. Here, perhaps, it is the more private nature of these artefacts, distributed only to the select few successful Olympians, that has allowed this out-of-favour visual vocabulary to retain its status as a signifier of sporting glory and honour.

Although the Olympic medal has traditionally been recognized as the sole prize awarded to athletes at the Games, during the early Olympic festivals of the modern era trophies were also occasionally offered to victors. Many of these, like the Olympic medals, were typically of a conventional design. One unique set of

Sèvres vase, awarded as a trophy to victors at the 1924 Paris Olympic Games.

prizes, however, is worthy of mention. To celebrate the Paris Games of 1924 the Sèvres Porcelain Factory manufactured a vase 1 metre (40 inches) high, based on a design by Octave-Denis-Victor Guillonnet, featuring gold olive branches set against a deep blue background. Four roundels, each representing different Olympic sports, decorated the side of the vase, which was put on display and offered for sale at the colossal sum of 22,500ff.[15] The following year the vase occupied a prominent position in the Sèvres display at the Paris International Exposition of Modern Industrial and Decorative Arts of 1925, the show famously credited with launching the Art Deco movement. More importantly, however, Sèvres also produced smaller versions of these vases, just 33 centimetres (13 inches) in height, which were offered as trophies to all winners at the Paris Games.[16] To reflect the diversity of sports practiced at the Games, several designs were produced, each bearing different roundels representing individual and team activities from athletics to rugby union. Many of the Sèvres Olympic vases have since entered museum collections as valuable examples of the exquisite art of the famous porcelain factory. A complete set of the trophies is also held at the Olympic Museum in Lausanne, where they certainly constitute one of the more unusual and beautifully designed victory trophies in Olympic history.

Carrying a Torch for the Olympics

Few events signal the imminence of an Olympic festival as evocatively as the staging of the Olympic torch relay. Like the award of medals, however, this ceremonial spectacle is very much a product of the modern era despite its invocation of a classical heritage. First introduced at the Berlin Games of 1936, the idea for a torch relay was initially proposed by Carl Diem, a German athlete, sports administrator and Olympic historian who had played an instrumental role in Germany's participation in the Olympic movement. Diem was not the first person to recognize the symbolic value of associating an eternal flame with the Games. As early as 1912, Coubertin had metaphorically

invoked the concept of Olympic fire in a speech at a banquet during the Stockholm Games when he declared, 'a great people has received the torch of the Olympiads from your hands and has thereby undertaken to preserve and if possible to quicken its precious flame'.[17] Further, the first official Olympic flame had been kept burning in Wils's modernist tower throughout the duration of the Amsterdam Games of 1928. Diem's idea, however, was dramatically to increase the significance of the Olympic flame by introducing a ceremony whereby this would not only be lit at ancient Olympia, but also carried by thousands of athletes to the destination of the Games. From this point on, the torch relay became one of the most effective advertising campaigns for any sporting event, and remains so to this day.

By commencing the torch relay at Olympia, Diem's performative spectacle openly exploited the associations between the ancient and modern Games. Here, however, the visual appearance of the torches also served to establish a link between the ancient world and modern German industry. Designed by Peter Wolf and Walter Lemcke, the Berlin torches were based on ancient columnar forms. Their sleek and elegant appearance, however, bears more than a passing affinity to the modernist designs of Bauhaus practitioners such as Marcel Breuer, Carl Jucker and Wilhelm Wagenfeld, despite the recent closure of the innovative design school by the National Socialist authorities. Manufactured from highly polished stainless steel and illuminated with magnesium flares, the torches were mass-produced by the German steelmaking firm Fried. Krupp AG, major players in the German armaments industry throughout the twentieth century. They were also notably designed both as highly functional, yet also ceremonial, artefacts. For example, the shaft of each of the over 3,500 torches produced was

Olympic torch designed for
the 1936 Berlin Olympic Games.

Ralph Lavers, Olympic torch designed for the 1948 London Olympic Games.

carefully decorated with an engraving of a map of the torch run, surmounted by an eagle clutching the Olympic rings. Further, a version of the torch was publicly displayed in a special Olympic train, as part of a travelling exhibition, as well as being exhibited at the Suermondt Museum in Aachen for the duration of the Games.[18] Thus, even before it had fulfilled its

original function in carrying the flame from Olympia to Berlin, the Olympic torch had already acquired a status as a valued design artefact worthy of public attention.

Despite its overt association with the Berlin Games, and thus the National Socialist regime, the torch relay was retained for the next Olympic Games in London in 1948. The torch used during the opening ceremony

Olympic torch designed for the 2008 Beijing Olympic Games.

at Wembley stadium, designed by Ralph Lavers, was similarly manufactured from high quality stainless steel and illuminated by magnesium flare. In contrast to its predecessor, however, the open bell and handle, designed to resemble a fluted column, made a more overt reference to the classical past. In this way, the classical heritage was once more being reclaimed from its earlier appropriation by the National Socialist regime. As economic conditions in post-war austerity Britain precluded the mass production of such torches, however, Lavers also produced a second, simpler and more budget-orientated torch design. Here cheaper aluminium replaced stainless steel while the use of longer burning solid fuel tablets enabled the extension of each stage in the relay and, as a consequence, a

significant reduction in the total number of torches required. This version was subsequently used by the 1,500 relay runners who carried the flame from Greece through Italy, Switzerland, France, Luxembourg and Belgium before landing on British shores.[19] Though lacking the elegance of the Berlin design, the London austerity torches of 1948 rapidly established a status as an iconic design, one notably re-used with only minor variations at the summer Games of Melbourne in 1956 and at the winter Games in Cortina D'Ampezzo and Squaw Valley in 1956 and 1960 respectively.

Since the 1960s, Olympic torch designs have evolved into a variety of ever more inventive forms. In 1964, for example, the torch comprised of little more than a cylindrical tube of stainless steel, thus reinforcing the minimalist design aesthetic widely deployed for the Tokyo Games. This also contrasted strikingly with the overly elaborate and squat design used for the Mexico City Games of 1968. Here, the torch bore an unfortunate resemblance to a police truncheon, an all too authoritarian symbol in the wake of the student riots that had taken place in Mexico City just ten days before the Games commenced.[20] It was not until the early 1990s that the Olympic torch design entered a new phase, as fashionable product designers such as Philippe Starck and André Ricard began to present ever stranger and more eccentric forms. Starck's strangely phallic torch used at the Albertville winter Games of 1992, for example, discarded all previous designs by eschewing symmetry and integrating both shaft and bell into one oddly swollen form. At the same time, Ricard's design for the Barcelona summer Games of the same year notably repeated this avoidance of symmetry, emphasizing the use of different components and materials and openly celebrating the constructed nature of the object. As the Official Report claimed, Ricard's torch was 'very Latin in character . . . a beautiful object in a sober style, unmistakably contemporary, and an attempt to reflect the best of Barcelona design'.[21] Both Starck's and Ricard's models effectively broke the mould for Olympic torch design, inspiring the use of a number of more innovative forms in recent years. These range from the environmentally friendly reference to a tree branch in the torch for the Lillehammer winter Games in 1994, to the colourful forms deployed for Sydney 2000, simultaneously referencing a boomerang and Sydney Opera House. The centrality of the Olympic torch also took on a new significance in Beijing in 2008 when a colossal replica of the hand-held torch, complete with its 'lucky clouds' motif, was lowered into position above the National Stadium to become the cauldron that would contain the Olympic flame for the duration of the Games.

This brief overview of various manifestations of Olympic design throughout the history of the modern Games suggests the possibility for further investigations into the role that both architecture and design practices have had, and continue to have, on our understanding of, and engagement with, the Olympic Games as a modern global phenomenon. Whether analysing the monumental stadium as festival centrepiece, the officially produced medal or torch, or even the humble mascot as mass reproduced on a variety of ephemera, these artefacts provide vital material evidence enabling us to explore, analyse and debate the ever-shifting signifying processes at play in conjunction with an event that is still widely perceived as the greatest sporting spectacle on earth.

CONCLUSION: AN OLYMPIC LEGACY?

Any visitor to the idyllic lakeside city of Lausanne in Switzerland in 1924 would have found a new tourist opportunity available to them. On Sundays they could visit the Villa Mon Repos, official headquarters of the IOC, and here see works of art, trophies, medals, diplomas and other assorted paraphernalia related to the Olympic Games, all from the private collection of Pierre de Coubertin. As founder of the Games, Coubertin had long held aspirations for the formation of an official Olympic Museum and worked on this project up until his death in 1937.[1] Yet despite his enthusiasm, Coubertin's museum attracted few visitors and remained a minor enterprise occupying limited space at the Villa Mon Repos up until its closure in the 1960s. From this point onwards, however, plans for a bigger and grander museum were regularly mooted and provisional spaces were found in Lausanne to display the IOC's growing collection and temporary exhibitions throughout the 1970s and '80s. It would not be until 1993, however, that a new museum would finally open. Situated on the Quai d'Ouchy, this five-floor modernist villa, surrounded by a sculpture park, has subsequently become the centrepiece for the preservation and public display of both visual and material culture artefacts related to the history of the Olympic Games.

Notably, the Olympic Museum in Lausanne is currently far from being the only museum dedicated to the history of the Games. In recent years Olympic Museums have begun to pop up in cities throughout the world so that today there are approximately 75 such museums in operation.[2] Several of these, such as the Lake Placid Winter Olympic Museum, the Seoul Olympic Museum, the Fundació Barcelona Olímpica and the Centennial Olympic Games Museum in Atlanta, Georgia, are notably based in former host cities. Here, they form part of an enduring cultural legacy, preserving the memory of individual Olympic festivals. Other major host cities have incorporated Olympic material into their national or local sports museums, many of which are situated on the site of former Games (for example, in Amsterdam, Helsinki and Melbourne).[3] Similar museums have also been built in places with less direct links to Olympic history, such as the Olympic Museum in Harare, Zimbabwe, while others are currently being planned for Israel, Kuwait and Qatar. This global expansion of Olympic museums provides an increased opportunity for new generations of sport and cultural historians to engage with and analyse a rich body of fascinating material that can provide insights into the ways that the Olympic movement as a whole has impacted upon society, from its first speculative steps in the late nineteenth century, to its initial growth in the early twentieth century to its maturity in our own age.

ArcelorMittal Orbit, designed by Anish Kapoor with Cecil Balmond; supported by Arup with Ushida Findlay Architects.

In 2012 London will become the first city to have hosted the summer Olympic Games on three separate occasions, and to mark this historic moment a number of cultural projects have been planned.[4] The most famous of these is the erection of a permanent monument to the Games, designed by Turner Prize-winning artist Anish Kapoor. The 115-metre (377-foot) tubular steel tower, officially named the ArcelorMittal Orbit, but dubbed the Colossus of Stratford even before its completion, is designed to allow visitors to ascend to an elevated platform and thus experience spectacular views over London. Commenting on the project in March 2010, London Mayor Boris Johnson claimed: 'Long after the Games are over, our aim is to have a stunning spectacle in east London that will be recognised around the world . . . Anish Kapoor's inspired art work will truly encapsulate the energy and spirit of London during the Games and, as such, will become the perfect iconic cultural legacy.'[5] The circular forms deployed in Kapoor's tower can be read as alluding to the Olympic rings. Other than this, however, the monument makes little reference to Olympic history or tradition.

Other planned events will celebrate Olympic history more overtly. For example, for the duration of the Games, the Royal Opera House in Covent Garden will host an exhibition entitled 'Olympic Journey: The Story of the Games'. Among the artefacts on display will be all the medals and torches from past Games, loaned by the Olympic Museum in Lausanne.

Although some initial proposals discussed the possibility of integrating museum space into the official stadium at Stratford, to date there appear to be no plans to build a permanent Olympic Museum in London. This is, in many respects, a pity, not least given the capital's rich Olympic heritage. Nonetheless, the staging of the Olympic Games in London 2012 will be another staging post in the history of the Games and will doubtless provide a rich opportunity for historians to analyse the ever-evolving cultural image and impact of the Olympics. Here, from both

a sporting and a wider socio-political perspective, a number of questions remain to be answered. For example, will China continue to dominate Olympic sports in the wake of the propaganda coup that was Beijing 2008? And how will the West, not least the United States, respond to this new challenge to sporting hegemony? Further, in the image-conscious, media driven world of today how will the organizers of the London Games follow the spectacular Chinese example and where will London 2012 fit in the historical pantheon of Olympic festivals? Whatever the answers to these questions might be one thing remains certain. Our historical understanding of the significance of the spectacle that will be London 2012 will depend not simply on the Games themselves, but also, and perhaps to a greater extent, on the ways that the event is documented and mediated to wider audiences through multiple forms of visual culture.

Torch design for the Olympic Games in London 2012.

REFERENCES

Introduction: Olympic Visions

1 Sports reporter Paul Kelso simply described this as 'the biggest event in the world', *Guardian* (8 August 2008). Hollywood director Stephen Spielberg, who had earlier been involved in the project, described Zhang's ceremony as nothing less than 'the greatest show on earth'. Stephen Spielberg, 'Person of the Year 2008: Runners-Up, Zhang Yimou', *Time* (17 December 2008).

2 *Official Report of the Beijing 2008 Olympic Games: Ceremonies and Competitions*, vol. II (Beijing, 2008), p. 77.

3 The Beijing Games are recorded as the Games of the 29th Olympiad, as no Games were held in 1916, 1940 and 1944 as a consequence of war.

4 See Mike Huggins and Mike O'Mahony, 'Prologue: Extending Study of the Visual in the History of Sport', *The International Journal of the History of Sport*, XXVIII/8 (2011), pp. 1089–104.

5 See, for example, Jean-Yves Guillain, *Art et Olympisme: Histoire du concours de peinture* (Paris, 2004).

1 Imaging the Ancient Olympics

1 Allen Guttmann, *The Olympics: A History of the Modern Games* (Champaign, IL, 1992), p. 14.

2 John J. MacAloon, *This Great Symbol: Pierre de Coubertin and the Origins of the Modern Olympic Games* (Chicago, IL, and London, 1981), pp. 164–79.

3 Ibid., p. 171.

4 Ibid., pp. 45–7.

5 David C. Young, *The Modern Olympics: A Struggle for Revival* (Baltimore, MD, 1996), p. 1.

6 Nigel Spivey, *The Ancient Olympics* (Oxford, 2004), p. 203.

7 For a compendium of classical writers on Greek sport and the Olympics in particular, see Stephen G. Miller, *Arete: Greek Sports from Ancient Sources* (Berkeley, CA, 1991).

8 William Shakespeare, *Henry VI, Part 3*, act 2, scene 3.

9 Christopher Whitfield, *Robert Dover and the Cotswold Games* (Evesham, 1962), p. 110.

10 This famous quotation, widely associated with Winckelmann, was included in his *Gedanken . . . (Thoughts on the Imitation of Greek Works in Painting and Sculpture)*, first published in 1755. It was first translated into English as 'noble simplicity and sedate grandeur' by Henry Fuseli in his translation of Winckelmann's text in 1765 under the title *Reflections on the Painting and Sculpture of the Greeks*.

11 M. I. Finlay and H. W. Pleket, *The Olympic Games: The First Thousand Years* (London, 1976), pp. 2–3.

12 Richard D. Mandell, *The First Modern Olympics* (Berkeley, CA, 1976); John J. MacAloon, *This Great Symbol*; Joachim Rühl, *Die Olympischen Spiele Robert Dovers* (Heidelberg, 1975).

13 Young, *The Modern Olympics*, p. 1.

14 Ibid., p. 3.

15 Ibid., p. 4.

16 Zappas was born in Northern Epirus, at that time under Ottoman rule, now Albania. Although he spent much of his life living in Bucharest in Romania, Zappas's sense of national affiliation was always on the side of Greece. During the War of Greek Independence of 1821, Zappas had fought alongside his fellow Greeks and later claimed he had been wounded five times.

17 Young, *The Modern Olympics*, p. 46.

18 At Olympia, the five events were: running, jumping, discus throwing, javelin throwing and wrestling. At Much Wenlock the five pentathlon events were: foot hurdle race, running high leap, running long leap, putting a weight of 16 kg (35 lb) and climbing a 17-metre (55-feet) rope.

19 Young, *The Modern Olympics*, p. 136.

1/2 (2003), p. 192.

19 Interview with Kon Ichikawa, *Tokyo Olympiad*, DVD (2002).

20 See David Scott Diffrient, 'An Olympic Omnibus: International Competition, Cooperation and Politics in *Visions of Eight*', *Film and History: An Interdisciplinary Journal of Film and Television Studies*, XXXV/2 (Spring 2005), pp. 19–28.

5 The Russians Are Coming! The Olympics and the Cold War

1 In 1908 Russia won a gold medal in figure skating and two silvers in Greco-Roman wrestling. Four years later they increased their overall haul by winning two silver medals (team pistol shooting and Greco-Roman Wrestling) and three bronzes (single skulls rowing, sailing and trap shooting).

2 James Riordan, *Sport in Soviet Society* (Cambridge, 1977), p. 66.

3 See André Gounot, 'Sport or Political Organization? Structures and Characteristics of the Red Sport International, 1921–1937', *Journal of Sport History*, XXVIII/1 (Spring 2001), pp. 23–39.

4 Mike O'Mahony, *Sport in the USSR: Physical Culture – Visual Culture* (London, 2006), p. 30.

5 *Izvestiya* (12 August 1928), p. 1.

6 James Riordan 'The Worker Sports Movement' in *The International Politics of Sport in the 20th Century*, ed. James Riordan and Arnd Krüger (London, 1995).

7 Jenifer Parks, 'Verbal Gymnastics: Sports, Bureaucracy and the Soviet Union's Entrance into the Olympic Games, 1946–52', in *East Plays West: Sport and the Cold War*, ed. Stephen Wagg and David L. Andrews (London and New York, 2007), p. 30.

8 Ibid., p. 31.

9 Vitaly Smirnov, 'Enter the Soviets', in *The Official History of the Olympic Games and the IOC: Athens to Beijing, 1894–2008*, ed. David Miller (Edinburgh, 2008), p. 133.

10 Allen Guttman, *The Olympics: A History of the Modern Games* (Champaign, IL, 1992), p. 98.

11 *The Official Report of the Organizing Committee for the Games of the XV Olympiad* (Helsinki, 1952), pp. 84–9. It might also be noted here that Soviet and Eastern European men and women were housed at the same venue, whereas a separate Women's Village was set up for other nations.

12 'Sport: The Strength of Ten', *Time* (21 July 1952).

13 'Sport: The Games Begin', *Time* (28 July 1952).

14 Ibid.

15 See Stefan Wiederkehr, '". . . if Jarmila Kratichvilova is the future of women's sports, I'm not sure I'm ready for it." Media, Gender and the Cold War', in *Euphoria and Exhaustion: Modern Sport in Soviet Culture and Society*, ed. Nikolaus Katzer, Sandra Budy, Alexandra Köhring and Manfred Zeller (Frankfurt and New York, 2010), p. 320.

16 Ibid., p. 320.

17 *Life* (7 October 1966), p. 63.

18 See Sarah Teetzel, 'Equality, Equity and Inclusion: Issues in Women and Transgendered Athletes' Participation at the Olympics' in *Cultural Imperialism in Action: Critiques in the Global Olympic Trust*, ed. Nigel Crowther, Michael Heine and Robert K. Barney (London, 2006), pp. 331–8.

19 The recent controversy surrounding the IAAF's (International Association of Athletics Federations) demand that South African athlete Caster Semenya undergo a gender test, provides further evidence that this issue still causes controversy in both the sporting and media worlds.

20 See, for example, the obituary of Irina Press published in *The Telegraph* (21 May 2004).

21 M. Ann Hall, *Feminism and Sporting Bodies* (Champaign, IL, 1996), p. 55.

22 Riordan, *Sport in Soviet Society*, pp. 18–20.

23 Ibid., p. 61.

24 Spitz won seven gold medals at the Munich Olympics, a record only recently surpassed by Michael Phelps's achievement in winning eight golds at the Beijing Games in 2008.

25 Jan Graydon, '"But It's More Than a Game. It's an Institution": Feminist Perspectives on Sport', *Feminist Review*, 13 (Spring 1983), p. 10.

26 Martha Duffy, 'Hello to a Russian Pixie', *Sports Illustrated* (19 March 1973), pp. 24–7.

27 Leigh Montville, 'Olga Korbut', *Sports Illustrated*, Special 40th Anniversary Issue (19 September 1994), p. 115.

28 Duffy, 'Hello to a Russian Pixie', p. 26.

29 *Sports Illustrated*, Special 40th Anniversary Issue (19 September 1994), p. 115.

30 John J. MacAloon, 'Double Vision: Olympic Games and American Culture', *The Kenyon Review*, IV/1 (Winter 1982), p. 111.

31 See Richard Pipes, 'Flight From Freedom: What

Russians Think and Want', *Foreign Affairs* (May/June 2004).

6 Olympic Transgressions: Drugs, Political Protest and Terrorism

1 Donald G. Kyle, *Sport and Spectacle in the Ancient World* (Oxford, 2007), p. 131.
2 Peter Levi, trans., *Pausanias, Guide to Greece: Southern Greece*, vol. II (London, 1979), pp. 259–63.
3 Ludwig Drees, *Olympia: Gods, Artists and Athletes* (London, 1968), p. 131. The bases of sixteen of these statues can still be found at the site of the ancient Games at Olympia.
4 Kyle, *Sport and Spectacle*, p. 131.
5 Charles J. P. Lucas, *The Olympic Games, 1904* (Official Report) (St Louis, MO, 1905), p. 46.
6 Ibid., p. 47.
7 Ibid., p. 46.
8 Ibid., p. 53.
9 Ibid., p. 52.
10 Ibid.
11 Judith Swaddling, *The Ancient Olympic Games* (Austin, TX, 1980), p. 49.
12 The only previous death during Olympic competition had been that of the Portuguese marathon runner, Francisco Lázaro, who died after collapsing during the race at the Games in Stockholm in 1912.
13 Rob Beamish and Ian Ritchie, 'The Spectre of Steroids: Nazi Propaganda, Cold War Anxiety and Patriarchal Paternalism', *International Journal of the History of Sport*, XXII/5 (September 2005), p. 785.
14 Ibid., p. 786.
15 *Toronto Sun* (26 September 1988), p. 1.
16 *Olympic Charter, in force as of 11 February 2010* (2010), p. 11: www.olympic.org/Documents/Olympic%20 Charter/Charter_en_2010.pdf (accessed 21 April 2011).
17 David K. Wiggins, ed., *African Americans in Sports*, vol. I (New York and London, 2004), p. 264.
18 Nancy J. Parezo, 'A "Special Olympics": Testing Racial Strength and Endurance at the 1904 Louisiana Purchase Exhibition', in *The 1904 Anthropology Days and Olympic Games: Sport, Race and American Imperialism*, ed. Susan Brownell (Lincoln, NB, 2008), p. 79.
19 J. E. Sullivan, *Spalding's Official Athletic Almanac for 1905, Special Olympic Number* (New York, 1905), p. 249.
20 Ibid.
21 Ibid., p. 259.

22 Allen Guttmann, *The Olympics: A History of the Modern Games* (Champaign, IL, 1992), p. 26.
23 Pierre de Coubertin, *Olympic Memoirs*, (Lausanne, 1997), p. 43.
24 William J. Baker, *Jesse Owens: An American Life* (New York, 1986), pp. 3–4.
25 Ibid., pp. 96–7.
26 Quoted in Larry Schwartz, 'Owens Pierced a Myth': http://espn.go.com/sportscentury/features/00016393.html (accessed 21 April 2011).
27 Robert K. Barney, 'A Research Note on the Origins of the Olympic Victory Podium', in *Global and Cultural Critique: Problematizing the Olympic Games, Fourth International Symposium for Olympic Research* (Ontario, 1998), p. 219.
28 Harry Edwards, *The Revolt of the Black Athlete* (New York, 1969), p. 104.
29 The Games of both Berlin (1936) and London (1948) had been televised live, but technological limitations meant that pictures were only distributed locally. The Tokyo Games of 1964 were the first to have live images beamed across the Pacific by satellite. From that point onwards, live television coverage of the Olympic Games has contributed enormously to the global appeal of the festival.
30 Douglas Hartmann, *Race, Culture, and the Revolt of the Black Athlete: The 1968 Olympic Protests and Their Aftermath* (Chicago, IL, 2003), p. 25.
31 See Jason Peterson, 'A "Race" for Equality: Print Media Coverage of the 1968 Olympic Protest by Tommie Smith and John Carlos', *American Journalism*, XXVI/2 (2009), p. 111.
32 *Time* (25 October 1968).
33 Hartmann, *Revolt of the Black Athlete*, p. 20.
34 At www.sjsu.edu/news/news_detail.jsp?id=1426 (accessed 23 April 2010).
35 Quoted in Michael Carlson's obituary of Peter Norman in the *Guardian* (5 October 2006).
36 Notably, when Norman died following a heart attack in 2006, both Smith and Carlos attended his funeral in Melbourne, delivered eulogies acted as pall-bearers. See Caroline Frost, 'The Other Man on the Podium', *BBC News Magazine*, online at: http://news.bbc.co.uk/1/ hi/7674157.stm (accessed 23 April 2011).
37 Simon Reeve, *One Day in September: The Full Story of the 1972 Munich Olympics Massacre and the Israeli Revenge Operation 'Wrath of God'* (London, 2005).
38 ABC television news coverage, 3.24 a.m. (Munich time)

(6 September 1972). See: www.youtube.com/ watch?v=w9HArGWgsm4 (accessed 19 April 2011).

39 Guttmann, *The Olympics*, pp. 138–9.

40 Ibid., p. 139.

41 Ibid., p. 140.

42 Among these are: a monument erected at the Fürstenfeldbruck airport, scene of the final moments of the siege; a figurative memorial in Tel Aviv; a Place of Memory in the Ben Shemen forest; and a memorial at the Wingate Institute for Physical Education and Sport in Netanya, the centre at which all of the 1972 Israeli Olympic team had trained prior to the Games.

7 Promoting the Games: Publicity and the Official Olympic Poster

1 *Official Report: The Olympic Games in 1896* (Athens, 1897), p. 28.

2 *Daily Mail* (17 July 1908), cited in Rebecca Jenkins, *The First London Olympics 1908* (London, 2008), pp. 142–3.

3 Olympic Charter, *in force as from 11 February 2010* (2010), p. 19: www.olympic.org/Documents/ Olympic%20Charter/Charter_en_2010.pdf (accessed 21 April 2011).

4 Bill Mallon and Ian Buchanan, 'To No Earthly King . . . The United States Flag Bearing Incident at the 1908 Olympic Games Opening Ceremony', *Journal of Olympic History*, VII/3 (1999), p. 22.

5 Ibid., pp. 21–8.

6 Keith Baker, *The 1908 Olympics* (Cheltenham, 2008), p. 27.

7 Stan Greenberg. 'What Special Relationship?', *Citius, Altius, Fortius*, III/1 (1995), pp. 27–9.

8 *Bystander* (5 August 1908), quoted in Jenkins, *The First London Olympics*, p. 242.

9 *Official Report of the Olympic Games of Stockholm 1912* (Stockholm, 1913), p. 266.

10 Ibid., p. 266.

11 Ibid., pp. 264–75.

12 Ibid., p. 262.

13 The Official Report noted that some nations refused to display the poster publicly as a consequence of its overt male nudity. Ibid., p. 277.

14 Roland Renson, *The Games Reborn: The VII Olympiad, Antwerp 1920* (Antwerp, 1996).

15 The conception of the poster has, however, been attributed to van der Ven's wife, the artist Martha van Kuyk. See Margaret Timmers, *A Century of Olympic Posters* (London, 2008), p. 31.

16 *Official Report of the Olympic Games, Berlin 1936*, vol. I (Berlin, 1936), p. 124.

17 Ibid.

18 *Official Report of the Organizing Committee for the XIV Olympiad* (London, 1948), p. 112.

19 For a full account of the various discoboli forms identified to date see Hara Thliveri, *Evidence for the Discobolos of Myron and its Place in Ancient Greek Art*, unpublished PhD Thesis, King's College, University of London (1996).

20 Timmers, *A Century of Olympic Posters*, p. 73.

21 *Official Report of the Organizing Committee for the Games of the XXth Olympiad*, vol. I (Munich, 1972), p. 207.

22 Other artists included in the Edition Olympia included Valerio Adami, Otmar Alt, Horst Antes, Shusaka Arakawa, Max Bill, Allan D'Arcangelo, Alan Davie, Piero Dorazio, Friedensreich Hundertwasser, Charles Lapicque, Jan Lenica, Marino Marini, Peter Phillips, Serge Poliakoff, Richard Smith, Fritz Winter, Paul Wunderlich and Victor Vasarely.

23 See Richard Stanton, *The Forgotten Olympic Art Competitions: The Story of the Olympic Art Competitions of the 20th Century* (Victoria, 2000).

24 *Official Report of the Olympic Games of Seoul, 1988*, vol. I (Seoul, 1989), p. 633.

25 Timmers, *A Century of Olympic Posters*, p. 129.

26 Ibid., p. 132.

8 Designs on the Olympics: From Stadia to Sporting Paraphernalia

1 Thomas Schmidt, 'Architecture at the Service of Sport: The Olympic Stadia from 1896 to 1936', *Olympic Review*, 226 (July 1986), pp. 397–402.

2 *The Official Report of the Organizing Committee of the Games of the XXth Olympiad, Munich 1972*, vol. II (Munich, 1972), pp. 32–59.

3 Having worked as an artistic consultant on the project, Ai Weiwei, a renowned critic of the Chinese authorities, subsequently denounced the National Stadium as a 'fake smile' designed to disguise the nation's social and political problems. See Evan Osnos, 'It's Not Beautiful: An Artist Takes on the System', *The New Yorker* (24 May 2010), p. 34.

4 Nicolai Ouroussoff, 'Olympic Stadium with a Design to Remember', *New York Times* (4 August 2008), p. D1.

5 Ibid.

6 Bill Henry, 'Smoky, Olympic Mascot Dead', *LA Times* (12 April 1934), n.p.

7 Ibid.

8 *The Games of the xth Olympiad, Los Angeles 1932, Official Report*, vol. I (Los Angeles, 1933), p. 258.

9 Tara Magdalinski, '"Cute Loveable Characters": The Place and Significance of Mascots in the Olympic Movement', *Olympika: The International Journal of Olympic Studies*, XIII (2004), p. 76.

10 *Official Report, Munich 1972*, p. 59.

11 Paula Welch, 'Cute Little Creatures: Mascots Lend a Smile to the Games', *Olympic Review*, 250–51 (September/October 1988), p. 438.

12 Christopher Booker, *The Games War: A Moscow Journal* (London, 1981), p. 200.

13 *Official Report of the Games of the XXV Olympiad, Barcelona 1992*, vol. III (Barcelona, 1992), p. 346.

14 'The Olympic Medals', *Olympic Review*, 34–5 (July/August 1970), p. 365.

15 Entrance to the Games (Stade Colombes) cost between 3 and 7ff at the time, which gives a rough indication of value. See *Temoins d'une certaine image des jeux*, exh. cat., Musée Olympique, Lausanne (2003), p. 56.

16 *Les jeux de la VIII Olympiade Paris 1924, Rapport Officiel* (Paris, 1924), p. 804.

17 Quoted in Walter Borgers, *Olympic Torch Relays, 1936–94* (Cologne, 1996), p. 12.

18 Ibid., pp. 28–9.

19 *The Official Report of the Organising Committee for the XIV Olympiad* (London, 1948), pp. 209–10.

20 The riots, at which hundreds of protesters were killed, were popularly dubbed the Tlatelolco Massacre.

21 *Official Report, Barcelona 1992*, p. 338.

Conclusion: An Olympic Legacy?

1 Marie-Pierre Huguenin, *Le Musée Olympique* (Lausanne, 1993), p. 7.

2 *Olympic Review*, 75 (2009), p. 18.

3 The Olympic Experience is an interactive multimedia exhibition situated in the Olympic Stadium in Amsterdam; The Sport Museum of Finland in Helsinki is situated in the former Olympic Stadium that hosted the 1952 summer Games; The National Sports Museum of Australia is situated at the Melbourne Cricket Ground which also operated as the main stadium for the summer Games of 1956.

4 Athens could also be said to have hosted the Games on three occasions if the Intercalary Games of 1906 are included, though official Olympic histories tend to exclude these.

5 At http://news.bbc.co.uk/1/hi/8597069.stm (accessed 24 May 2011).

SELECT BIBLIOGRAPHY

Arvin-Bérod, Alain, *Les Enfants d'Olympie, 1796–1896* (Paris, 1996)

Baker, Keith, *The 1908 Olympics* (Cheltenham, 2008)

Baker, William J., *Jesse Owens: An American Life* (New York, 1986)

Beamish, Rob, and Ian Ritchie, 'The Spectre of Steroids: Nazi Propaganda, Cold War Anxiety and Patriarchal Paternalism', *International Journal of the History of Sport*, XXII/5 (September 2005)

Blackman, Cally, *100 Years of Fashion Illustration* (London, 2007)

Blue, Adrianne, *Faster, Higher, Further: Women's Triumphs and Disasters at the Olympics* (London, 1988)

Booker, Christopher, *The Games War: A Moscow Journal* (London, 1981)

Borgers, Walter, *Olympic Torch Relays, 1936–94* (Cologne, 1996)

Braun, Marta, *Picturing Time: The Work of Étienne-Jules Marey, 1830–1904* (Chicago, IL, 1992)

Brownell, Susan, ed., *The 1904 Anthropology Days and Olympic Games: Sport, Race and American Imperialism* (Lincoln, NB, 2008)

Carpentier, Florence, and Jean-Pierre Lefèvre, 'The Modern Olympic Movement, Women's Sport and the Social Order During the Inter-War Period', *International Journal of the History of Sport*, XXIII/7 (November 2006)

Cayliff, Susan E., *Babe: The Life and Legend of Babe Didrikson Zaharias* (Chicago, IL, 1996)

de Coubertin, Pierre, *Olympic Memoirs*, (Lausanne, 1997)

——, *Pédagogie Sportive* (Paris, 1922)

Cropper, Corry, *Playing at Monarchy: Sport as Metaphor in Nineteenth-Century France* (Lincoln, NB, 2008)

Crowther, Nigel, Michael Heine and Robert K. Barney, eds, *Cultural Imperialism in Action: Critiques in the Global Olympic Trust* (London, 2006)

Davis, Mary E., *Ballets Russes Style: Diaghilev's Dancers and Paris Fashion* (London, 2010)

Downing, Taylor, 'The First Olympic Games on Reel', *Olympic Review*, 227 (September 1986)

Drees, Ludwig, *Olympia: Gods, Artists and Athletes* (London, 1968)

Drevon, André, *Alice Milliat: La pasionaria du sport féminin* (Paris, 2005)

——, *Les jeux olympiques oubliés: Paris 1900* (Paris, 2000)

Edwards, Harry, *The Revolt of the Black Athlete* (New York, 1969)

Engelmann, Larry, *The Goddess and the American Girl: The Story of Suzanne Lenglen and Helen Wills* (Oxford, 1988)

Epsy, Richard, *The Politics of the Olympic Games* (Berkeley and Los Angeles, CA, 1979)

Finlay, M. I., and H. W. Pleket, *The Olympic Games: The First Thousand Years* (London, 1976)

Gardiner, E. Norman, *Athletics of the Ancient World* (Oxford, 1930)

Gounot, André, 'Sport or Political Organization? Structures and Characteristics of the Red Sport International, 1921–1937', *Journal of Sport History*, XXVIII/1 (Spring 2001)

Graham, Cooper C., *Leni Riefenstahl and Olympia* (London, 1986)

Graydon, Jan, '"But It's More Than a Game. It's an Institution": Feminist Perspectives on Sport', *Feminist Review*, 13 (Spring 1983)

Greenberg, Stan, 'What Special Relationship?', *Citius, Altius, Fortius*, III/1 (1995)

Guillain, Jean-Yves, *Art et Olympisme: histoire du concours de peinture* (Paris, 2004)

Guttmann, Allen, *The Olympics: A History of the Modern Games* (Champaign, IL, 1992)

Hall, M. Ann, *Feminism and Sporting Bodies* (Champaign, IL, 1996)

Hampton, Janie, *The Austerity Olympics: When the Games Came to London in 1948* (London, 2008)

Hargreaves, Jennifer, *Heroines of Sport: The Politics of Difference and Identity* (London and New York, 2000)

——, *Sporting Females: Critical Issues in the History and Sociology of Women's Sports* (London, 1994)

Hartmann, Douglas, *Race, Culture, and the Revolt of the Black Athlete: The 1968 Olympic Protests and Their Aftermath* (Chicago, IL, 2003)

Hinton, David, *The Films of Leni Riefenstahl* (London, 2000)

Holt, Richard, *Sport and the British: A Modern History* (Oxford, 1989)

Huggins, Mike, and Mike O'Mahony, 'Prologue: Extending Study of the Visual in the History of Sport', *The International Journal of the History of Sport*, XXVIII/8 (2011)

Huguenin, Marie-Pierre, *Le Musée Olympique* (Lausanne, 1993)

Jenkins, Rebecca, *The First London Olympics, 1908* (London, 2008)

Katzer, Nikolaus, Sandra Budy, Alexandra Köhring and Manfred Zeller, eds, *Euphoria and Exhaustion: Modern Sport in Soviet Culture and Society* (Frankfurt and New York, 2010)

Kluge, Volker, ed., *The Pictures of the First Olympiad by Albert Meyer and other Photographers* (Berlin, 1996)

Kyle, Donald G., *Sport and Spectacle in the Ancient World* (Oxford, 2007)

Leigh, Mary, and Thérèse M. Bonin, 'The Pioneering Role of Madame Alice Milliat and the FSFI in Establishing International Trade and Field Competition for Women', *Journal of Sport History*, IV/1 (1977)

Lennartz, Karl, 'The 2nd International Olympic Games in Athens 1906', *Journal of Olympic History*, 10 (2001)

Leossi, Athena, S., *Nationalism and Classicism: The Classical Body as National Symbol in Nineteenth-century England and France* (London 1998)

Le sport s'expose: regard sur les collections du musée national du sport, exh. cat., Musée du sport, Paris (2008)

Levi, Peter, trans., *Pausanias, Guide to Greece: Southern Greece*, vol. II (London, 1979)

Llewelyn Smith, Michael, *Olympics in Athens, 1896* (London, 2004)

MacAloon, John J., 'Double Vision: Olympic Games and American Culture', *The Kenyon Review*, IV/1 (Winter 1982)

——, *This Great Symbol: Pierre de Coubertin and the Origins of the Modern Olympic Games* (Chicago, IL, and London, 1981)

——, Miguel de Moragas and Montserrat Llinés, eds, *Olympic Ceremonies: Historical Continuity and Cultural Exchange* (Barcelona and Lausanne, 1995)

Magdalinski, Tara, '"Cute Loveable Characters": The Place and Significance of Mascots in the Olympic Movement', *Olympika: The International Journal of Olympic Studies*, XIII (2004)

Mallon, Bill, and Ian Buchanan, 'To No Earthly King . . . The United States Flag Bearing Incident at the 1908 Olympic Games Opening Ceremony', *Journal of Olympic History*, VII/3 (1999)

Mandell, Richard D., *The First Modern Olympics* (Berkeley, CA, 1976)

——, *The Nazi Olympics* (London, 1972)

——, *Sport: A Cultural History* (New York, 1984)

Matthews, George R., *America's First Olympics: The St Louis Games of 1904* (Columbia, 2005)

Masumoto, Naofumi, and Gordon MacDonald, '"Tokyo Olympiad": Olympism Interpreted from the Conflict Between Artistic Representation and Documentary Film', *International Journal of Sport and Health Science*, I/2 (2003)

Miller, David, ed., *The Official History of the Olympic Games and the IOC: Athens to Beijing, 1894–2008* (Edinburgh, 2008)

Miller, Stephen G., ed., *Arete: Greek Sports from Ancient Sources* (Berkeley, CA, 1991)

Muller, Norbert, ed., *Pierre de Coubertin, 1863–1937: Olympism, Selected Writings* (Lausanne, 2000)

——, and Christian Hacker, eds, *Pierre Coubertin et les arts*, exh. cat., Lausanne (2008)

Musée Olympique, *Temoins d'une certaine image des jeux*, exh. cat., Lausanne (2003)

O'Mahony, Mike, *Sergei Eisenstein* (London, 2008)

——, *Sport in the USSR: Physical Culture – Visual Culture* (London, 2006)

Peterson, Jason, 'A "Race" for Equality: Print Media Coverage of the 1968 Olympic Protest by Tommie Smith and John Carlos', *American Journalism*, XXVI/2 (2009)

Polley, Martin, *The British Olympics: Britain's Olympic Heritage, 1612–2012* (London, 2011)

Poulton, Emma, and Martin Roderick, eds, *Sport in Films* (Oxford, 2008)

Reeve, Simon, *One Day in September: The Full Story of the 1972 Munich Olympics Massacre and the Israeli Revenge Operation 'Wrath of God'* (London, 2005)

Renson, Roland, *The Games Reborn: The VII Olympiad, Antwerp, 1920* (Antwerp, 1996)

Riefenstahl, Leni, *Olympia* (Cologne, 2002)

Riordan, James, *Sport in Soviet Society* (Cambridge, 1977)

——, 'The Worker Sports Movement' in James Riordan and Arnd Krüger, *The International Politics of Sport in the 20th Century* (London, 1995)

——, and Arnd Krüger, *The International Politics of Sport in the 20th Century* (London, 1995)

Rowe, David, *Critical Readings: Sport, Culture and the Media* (Maidenhead, 2009)

Rühl, Joachim, *Die Olympischen Spiele Robert Dovers* (Heidelberg, 1975)

Schmidt, Thomas, 'Architecture at the Service of Sport: The Olympic Stadia from 1896 to 1936', *Olympic Review*, 226 (July 1986)

Schweinbenz, Amanda, '"Let the Games Begin!" Analysis of the Print Media's Contribution to Masculine Sports Hegemony at the 1932 Olympic Games', *The Global Nexus Engaged, Sixth International Symposium for Olympic Research* (October 2002)

Scott Diffrient, David, 'An Olympic Omnibus: International Competition, Cooperation and Politics', *Visions of Eight', Film and History: An Interdisciplinary Journal of Film and Television Studies*, xxxv/2 (Spring 2005)

Spivey, Nigel, *The Ancient Olympics* (Oxford, 2004)

Stanton, Richard, *The Forgotten Olympic Art Competitions: The Story of the Olympic Art Competitions of the 20th Century* (Victoria, 2000)

Sullivan, J. E., *Spalding's Official Athletic Almanac for 1905, Special Olympic Number* (New York, 1905)

Swaddling, Judith, *The Ancient Olympic Games* (Austin, TX, 1980)

Thliveri, Hara, *Evidence for the Discobolos of Myron and its Place in Ancient Greek Art*, unpublished PhD Thesis, King's College, University of London (1996)

Timmers, Margaret, *A Century of Olympic Posters* (London, 2008)

de Wael, Herman, 'Olympic or Not? A Discussion about the Status of Events of 1900 and 1904', *Journal of Olympic History*, xi/1 (January 2003)

Wagg, Stephen, and David L. Andrews, eds, *East Plays West: Sport and the Cold War* (London and New York, 2007)

Wallechinsky, David, *The Complete Book of the Olympic Games* (London, 2008)

Welch, Paula, 'Cute Little Creatures: Mascots Lend a Smile to the Games', *Olympic Review*, 250–1 (September/October 1988)

Whitfield, Christopher, *Robert Dover and the Cotswold Games* (Evesham, 1962)

Wiggins, David K., ed., *African Americans in Sports* (New York and London, 2004)

Young, David C., *The Modern Olympics: A Struggle for Revival* (Baltimore, MD, 1996)

ACKNOWLEDGEMENTS

It is a widely deployed convention in acknowledgements pages to use the phrase 'without whom this book could not have been completed'. Typically this refers to the academic colleagues, librarians and archival staff who have assisted a researcher in bringing a project such as this one to fruition. In this instance, however, I wish to beg the indulgence of these aforementioned specialists to prioritize an entirely different group of people, to whom I offer my profound gratitude. In July 2009, as I was about to embark on research for this project, I was unfortunate enough to fall seriously ill. For several weeks my continued existence lay entirely in the hands of a group of quite extraordinary doctors, nurses and support staff at the Bristol Royal Infirmary, many of whom fought day and night to keep me from shuffling off this mortal coil. Over the next two months, these extraordinary staff, many of whom remained nameless or modestly introduced themselves only by their first name, and in any case are far too numerous to name here individually, tended me back to health and gave me what I now regard, and value on a daily basis, as my second life. Thus I, along with so many countless others, both owe and acknowledge a lifelong debt that can never be repaid to the wonderful, highly professional and dedicated medical and support staff of the NHS; specifically the Intensive Care and High Dependency Units of the BRI, the Cardiac Care Unit at the Bristol Heart Foundation, as well as the Physiotherapy Unit and Wards 51 and 53. I think it is only fair to say, quite literally, that without these individuals much more than this book most definitely would not have been completed.

In addition to the medical staff, one other individual played an immeasurable role in my recovery, and thus enabled me to complete this book. My wonderful wife Claire sat by my bedside throughout the darkest days and nights of my illness, sometimes 24 hours a day, reading my favourite books and poems to me, playing my favourite music to me, and constantly reassuring me, even as I lay in a coma, that everything would be alright. She was, of course, right, though I have no doubt that without that support I would not be here today to acknowledge this. Sometimes saying thank you, simply doesn't hack it!

I also extend my gratitude to the Leverhulme Trust, and in particular Jean Cater, whose flexibility and understanding at this time allowed me to delay commencing a Research Fellowship until I was fully able to take advantage of this opportunity. This Fellowship has been instrumental in enabling me to work on this project. Finally I wish to thank Marie-Laure Lauria of the Olympic Museum in Lausanne for her patience, understanding and guidance in acquiring many of the images included in this book.

PHOTO ACKNOWLEDGEMENTS

The author and publishers wish to express their thanks to the below sources of illustrative material and/or permission to reproduce it:

Photos akg-images: pp. 13, 18 (foot); photo akg-images / Rabatti-Doming: p. 16 (foot); © Arup: p. 156; photo © Austrian Archives / Corbis: p. 70; © 2012 Banco de México Diego Rivera Frida Kahlo Museums Trust, Mexico, D.F. / DACS: p. 54 (lower right); photos © Bettmann / Corbis: pp. 58, 96, 112, 113, 115; photo © Manuel Blondeau / Corbis: p. 61; The British Library, London (photos © The British Library Board): pp. 66, 124; The British Museum, London (photos © The Trustees of the British Museum): pp. 16 (top), 17, 46; photos © British Pathe: p. 64; photo courtesy of the artist (Grisha Bruskin): p. 101; Calder Foundation, New York: p. 53 © 2012 Calder Foundation, New York / DACS, London (photo Calder Foundation, New York / Art Resource, NY © DACS); from *The Century* (November 1896): pp. 29, 36; from *Concours internationaux d'exercises physiques et de sports*, vol. II (Paris, 1900): p. 40; photos © Corbis: pp. 49, 75, 134; photo Ralph Crane / Time Life Pictures / Getty Images: p. 87; photo David Berger National Memorial: p. 121; from *Femina* (15 August 1912): p. 50; photo © Getty Images: p. 119; from Ludwig Gottfried, *Historische Chronica* (Frankfurt am Main, 1630): p. 13; photo © Hulton-Deutsch Collection / Corbis: p. 44; photo © Sadequi Hussain / Shutterstock: p. 15; photos © 2011 International Olympic Committee – all rights reserved: pp. 10, 32, 37, 40, 77, 78, 79, 104, 109, 110, 126, 128, 130, 131, 133, 136, 137 (© Lance Wyman), 139, 145, 146, 147, 148, 149, 151, 152, 153; photo © Gilbert Iundt: p. 102; from *Izvestiya*, 12 August 1928: p. 82; photo Mark Kauffman: p. 91 (right); photo © KPA / ZUMA / Corbis: p. 62; photo Latvian National Museum of Art, Riga: p. 85; photos © Leni Riefenstahl Produktion: pp. 71, 72, 73; photo © Theodore Liasi / ZUMA Press / Corbis: p. 157; Library of Congress, Washington, DC (Prints and Photographs Division): pp. 41, 69, 74, 105, 129; from *Life* magazine, 28 July 1952: p. 88; photo © Ma Hailin / Xinhua Press / Corbis: p. 144; Mary Evans Picture Library: p. 63; Museo Archeologico Nazionale, Tarquinia, Italy: p. 16 (foot); photo Museum of London: p. 122; from *Die Olympischen Spiele in Berlin und Garmisch-Partenkirchen* (Hamburg and Berlin, 1936): p. 129; photos Mike O'Mahony: pp. 19, 117, 142; from *Le Petit Journal* (26 April 1896): p. 34; photo © Popperfoto / Getty Images: p. 47 (left); private collections: 26, 68 (top), 84; from *Punch* (18 April 1896): p. 35; photos Roger-Viollet, courtesy Rex Features: pp. 34, 43; Royal Society of Arts, London (photo © The Royal Society of Arts, London): p. 18 (top); photo Jean-Yves Ruszniewski / TempSport / Corbis: p. 102; photo © Sampics / Corbis: p. 6; from *Scribner's Magazine* (September 1896): pp. 30, 31; from *The Sketch*, XLIII / 808 (July 1908): p. 66; from *Le Sportif* magazine (25 August 1922): p. 56; photos *Sports Illustrated* / Getty Images: pp. 95, 99; from J. Sullivan, *Spalding's Official Athletic Almanac for 1905: Special Olympic Number, Containing the Official Report of the Olympic Games of 1904* (New York, 1905): pp. 109, 110; photo Templar52: p. 28; photos Time Life Pictures / Getty Images: pp. 89, 90, 91; from *The Times* (25 July 1935): p. 68 (foot); from *The Toronto Sun*, 26 September 1988 (Sun Media Corporation): p. 106; photo © Underwood & Underwood / Corbis: p. 51 (left); from *Vanity Fair* (August 1932): p. 54 (top left); from *La Vie au Grand Air*: pp. 47 right (1900), 51 right (1921); from *La Vie Parisienne* (1921): p. 63; from Matthew Walbancke, *Annalia Dubrensia* (London, 1636): p. 14; photos Wenlock Olympian Society: pp. 21, 22, 23; photo Wikifrits: p. 59; photo © Adam Woolfitt / Corbis: p. 143; design Lance Wyman – Art Direction Pedro Ramirez Vasquez, Eduardo Terrazas: p. 137.

INDEX